One of the earliest and and most compelling educator voices of discontent was Ian Jukes. For many years, he has told the story of education in a time of rapid change to audiences all over the world. He has helped us to fully understand the vision of an education institution that no longer fits it's time, and has articulated a new vision that reinvents the institution within the context of new technologies, a new information landscape, a new generation (species) of learner, and the opportunities of rapidly changing times.

In *Living On the Future Edge: Windows on Tomorrow*, Jukes, along with Ted McCain and Lee Crockett, paint the picture of an industry that, like others, seems unable and unwilling to look beyond its own image of itself. They describe the concept of paradigm paralysis, where schooling's mission, model, and method have become so locked within an industrial mode that it has practically ignored the swift and profound shifts that have been occurring around it during the past several decades.

Jukes, McCain, and Crockett help readers to examine their own paradigms and then to understand the challenges of looking straight (linear thinking) into a future that is changing faster and faster, and building on itself at ever increasing speeds (exponential thinking). The authors suggest a split screen approach to teaching and learning, with a focus on the realities of the present while aiming to a future that hasn't happened yet—throwing the ball to where the receiver is going to be, to use their football metaphor.

Across a series of chapters, readers witness several roadways of change through the exponential growth of computer processing power, bandwidth for communication, the overwhelming growth of information, and the idea that these changes might actually be harnessed as opportunities rather than feared for their disruptive effects.

The authors help us map out new paradigms for schooling that teach for our children's future, rather than for our past. It is a learning that is less defined by what our children can be taught, and much more by what they can learn within teacher-crafted learning experiences that are personal, meaningful, and intrinsically valuable. Readers are also helped to answer questions that will almost certainly be nagging at them throughout *Living on the Future Edge*: What do our children need to be learning to be ready for this kind of future? What are the basic skills of the 21st century? The answers are clear, and they are obvious to those who let go of their old paradigms.

As the institution of education changes, so too will the roles of educators, and readers of this book will explore the nature of some of these changes. What is often described a being the "guide on the side" instead of the "sage on the stage" is described in details that will both inform and inspire. This book helps educators to realize a new vision of teaching, learning, and the culture that they happen in, devoted not to a stale institution, but to the needs of today's children, the brand new world that they are growing up in, and a future that we can no longer describe.

Join Jukes, McCain, and Crockett for an enlightening look through a window to the future.

David Warlick

Ted McCain

Ted McCain is an educator who has taught high school students for 25 years. He has been an innovator and pioneer in technology education. He has designed courses for his school district and the province of British Columbia in computer science, data processing, desktop publishing, computer networking, web site design, digital animation, digital film effects, and sound engineering. In 1997, he received the Prime Minister's Award for Teaching Excellence. Ted has written or co-written seven books on the future, effective teaching, educational technology, and graphic design. His focus is on the impact on students and learning from the astounding changes taking place in the world today as a consequence of technological development.

Ian Jukes

Ian Jukes is the founder and director of the InfoSavvy Group, an international consulting firm. He has been a teacher at all grade levels; a school, district, and provincial administrator; a university instructor; and a national and international consultant. But first and foremost, Ian is a passionate educational evangelist. To date he has written or co-written 14 books and 9 educational series and has had more than 200 articles published in various journals around the world. From the beginning, Ian's focus has been on the compelling need to restructure our educational institutions so that they become relevant to the current and future needs of children or, as David Thornburg writes, "to prepare them for their future and not just our past." Ian can be reached at iajukes@me.com.

Lee Crockett

Lee Crockett is a national award-winning designer, marketing consultant, entrepreneur, artist, author, and international keynote speaker. He is the director of media for the InfoSavvy Group and the managing partner of the 21st Century Fluency Project. He has co-authored three books with writers and educators Ian Jukes and Ted McCain. Lee is a "just-in-time learner" who is constantly adapting to the new programs, languages, and technologies associated with today's communications and marketing media. Understanding the need for balance in our increasingly digital lives, Lee has lived in Kyoto, Japan, where he studied Aikido and tea ceremony, as well as Florence, Italy, where he studied painting at the Accademia D'Arte.

I dedicate this book to Heather. I cannot begin to describe how her support, interest, and thoughtful criticism have contributed to my thinking and writing.

Ted McCain

I dedicate this book to the memory of my Dad, Arthur Jukes, my Mother, Margaret Jukes, and my brother, John Jukes. We miss you all. And to my son, Kyler, and his beautiful wife, Natalee. And last but certainly not least, to my long-distance NZ Skype buddy, Nicky Mohan.

Ian Jukes

I dedicate this book to Tomomi, with whom I am so blessed to share this exponential future.

Lee Crockett

Many thanks to Dr. Jason Ohler, Andrew Churches, Nicky Mohan, Ross Crockett, Kim Ibach, Doug Johnson, Nikos Theodosakis, Dr. James Cisek, Andrew Croll, Deb Stollenwerk, Meg Ormiston, Dr. Matt McClure, Mick Harper, Leigh Peake, Belinda Thresher, Tomomi Watanabe, Mae Crockett, Heather McCain, and Lori Anderson.

21st Century Fluency Project

co-published with

CORWIN
A SAGE Company

Cover Photo: ©iStockphoto.com/PeskyMonkey

For information:

21st Century Fluency Project Inc.
1685 Smithson Place
Kelowna BC Canada V1Y 8N5
www.fluency21.com

ISBN 978-1-4499-7552-6(pbk.)
EAN 9781449975524

Acquisitions Editor: Debra Stollenwerk
Editorial, Production, and Indexing: Abella Publishing Services, LLC
Typesetter: Ross Crockett
Cover Designer: Lee Crockett

Table of Contents

21st Century Fluency Project

The 21st Century Fluency Project is about moving vision into practice through the process of investigating the impact on our society and our children over the last few decades, learning how we in education must evolve, and, finally, committing to changes at the classroom level.

Living on the Future Edge is the first book in our 21st Century Fluency Series. We face a world on the move, and education needs to react. A series of six books, as well as related supporting materials, has been developed in order to answer five essential questions that teachers will ask when considering how educators and education must respond to the profound developments that are being experienced in the world at large.

Why Do I Have to Change?

Living on the Future Edge
The Impact of Global Exponential Trends on Education in the 21st Century

In this book, we discuss the power of paradigm to shape our thinking, the pressure that technological development is putting on our paradigm for teaching and learning, six exponential trends in technological development that we can't ignore, what these trends means for education, new skills for students, new roles for teachers, and scenarios of education in the future.

Understanding the Digital Generation
Teaching and Learning in the New Digital Landscape

This book examines the effects that digital bombardment from constant exposure to electronic media has on kids in the new digital landscape and considers the profound implications this holds for the future of education. What does the latest neuroscientific and psychological research tell us about the role of intense and frequent experiences on the brain, particularly the young and impressionable brain?

Based on the research, what inferences can we make about kids' digital experiences and how these experiences are rewiring and reshaping their cognitive processes? More important, what are the implications for teaching, learning, and assessment in the new digital landscape?

How can we reconcile these new developments with current instructional practices, particularly in a climate of standards and accountability driven by high-stakes testing for all? What strategies can we use to appeal to the learning preferences and communication needs of digital learners while at the same time honoring our traditional assumptions and practices related to teaching, learning, and assessment?

Where Do I Start?

The Digital Diet
Today's Digital Tools In Small Bytes

This book offers bite-sized, progressively challenging projects to introduce the reader to the digital landscape of today. This is the world of our children and students. *The Digital Diet* will help readers shed pounds of assumptions and boost their digital metabolism to help keep pace with these kids by learning to use some simple yet powerful digital tools.

How Can I Teach Differently?

Teaching for Tomorrow
Teaching Content and Problem-Solving Skills

A key book in this series, *Teaching for Tomorrow* is a practical book for teachers struggling with teaching 21st-century problem-solving skills while still covering the content in the curriculum guide. The book outlines a new teaching approach that significantly shifts the roles of the teacher and the student in learning. These new roles facilitate student ownership of learning. *Teaching for Tomorrow* also outlines the 4D problem-solving process, a process that students must know intimately if they are to become independent problem solvers.

What Would This Teaching Look Like in My Classroom?

Literacy Is Not Enough
21st Century Fluencies for the Digital Age

It is no longer enough that we educate only to the standards of the traditional literacies. To be competent and capable in the 21st century requires a completely different set of skills—the 21st-century fluencies—that are identified and explained in detail in this book. The balance of the book introduces our framework for integrating these fluencies in our traditional curriculum.

Curriculum Integration Kits

These kits are subject- and grade-specific publications designed to integrate the teaching of 21st-century fluencies into today's curriculum and classroom. Included are detailed learning scenarios, resources, rubrics, and lesson plans with suggestions for high-tech, low-tech, or no-tech implementation. Also identified is the traditional content covered, as well as the standards and 21st-century fluencies each project covers.

The 21st Century Fluency Project Web Site

www.fluency21.com

Our web site contains supplemental material that provides support for classroom teachers who are implementing 21st-century teaching. The site lets teachers access pre-made lesson plans that teach traditional content along with 21st-century fluencies. The site also provides teachers with a blank template for designing their own lessons for teaching 21st-century fluencies. There are also other shared resources and a forum for additional collaboration and support.

How Can We Design Effective Schools for the 21st Century?

Teaching the Digital Generation

No More Cookie Cutter High Schools

The world has changed. Young people have changed. But the same underlying assumptions about teachers, students, and instruction that have guided high school design for a hundred years continue to shape the way high schools are designed today. In fact, so much is assumed about the way a high school should look, that new schools are created from a long-established template without question. Strip away the skylights, the fancy foyers, and the high-tech PA systems, and new schools being constructed today look pretty much the way they did when most adults went to school.

This is a mismatch with reality. We need new designs that incorporate what we have learned about young people and how they learn best. This book outlines a new process for designing high schools and provides descriptions of several new models for how schools can be configured to better support learning.

 # Foreword

There's today, and there's the future.

We grow up with expectations of how life works. We live in, and adapt to, the guides and resources that will lead us to jobs and money and homes and families. All around we see clues as to how life works. We see what we need to do to achieve expectable results. Life ahead seems very nice for all.

And then, things change a lot.

Perhaps our homeland is uprooted in war, and there are no longer homes or jobs. It's easy to say that we have to adapt, but hard to actually do. The change in our lifetime due to the emergence of inexpensive and powerful electronic tools has left us in a similar situation. I look at all the activities I do every day on my computer, and wonder how we ever did them without these tools.

Let's look at some of this drastic change. With today's computers and the Internet, we now manage our various bank accounts and other online accounts. When we need information, instead of asking the smart people around us, we ask someone who's' name starts with G (that's a joke for Google or God). Real phone calls with voice are being replaced by text, which invades space more politely. We establish friendships with countless people we've never met. We spend countless hours watching funny and creative videos on YouTube. We create our own multimedia presentations. The list goes on and on.

This change in our lifetimes (for those of us who remember the 'before' ages) seems like something that never before happened in such a short time. We have trouble adapting, often following the kids' examples. I know that's true for me. The changes in our future seem insurmountable. Newspapers are being replaced for news and classified ads. CD's have become more of a 'gift' or 'memory' item than actual music. DVD's provide much of our video entertainment, yet they are also being supplanted (here bandwidth permits) by online viewing and purchasing. Some predict the demise of physical books in lieu of electronic ones. We want to deny such major change, even as we see it being unstoppable, like a huge bulldozer knocking obstacles down.

We fight the inevitable and visible change because we are human. We have memories of how things like education are done. Even though the primary academic tool of our life is now the personal computer (and Internet), we most often structure schools the same as before. We have the same organizational roles, and teach the same number of hours of the same material as before. It's time that we use modern computer technology to change the paradigms of education.

When my children were young, I found that they were more attracted to educationally-oriented programs when the computers better resembled real people. Every time the graphics got more real and the voices sounded like live people, the more my kids were attracted to the computer, as though it was a friend. You get used to one level and then the computers get better and attract you again. We've made incredible progress, but still have a long way to go to make the computer indistinguishable from a human. But it will happen, and probably accidentally, without our trying to.

The number of interment nodes is of an order of magnitude the number of neurons in our brains. The number of Internet connections is of an order of magnitude the number of synapses in our brains. And now we ask our tough questions of a computer, rather than of a human. It's as though a form that we call intelligence emerged without any conscious attempt to create it. Such is often the behavior when there are enough small things that swarm by sets of simple rules.

The future is in the hands of the students. It's in the values and social methodologies and ways of arriving at solutions that define the world as we know it. Yet education seems like a stagnant part of the new digital world. This is true for many reasons. Teachers didn't learn on computers, and usually aren't tech leaders. Students regress to the expectations of their teachers, and don't use computers as fully as they could. And money is always a problem. Those without children in schools are sort of against those with children in schools. It's like the old versus the young. But money comes from votes in our system, and adults get a vote while children do not. A family of 5 gets no more votes than a family of 2, and the result is less money for schools than they deserve.

I look at young students and how they love using computers, and I think of a paradigm shift for a class of 30 young students. Today, as always before, the presentation from a teacher is fixed for all in the class. They all get the same presentation of material. Then a test determines a variable grade that sorts the students out. If you are on the low end of early grades, you don't value your education as much, since it seems you can never compete with the brains.

But imagine 30 computers acting as 30 teachers. Each student can be progressing at different speeds for different subjects, depending upon their interests and abilities. All of the computers have programs that are set to teach until the student is competent in every subject. The student decides to have straight A's and the computer will guarantee that level of learning, but it will take varying amounts of time for different students. The result (grade) is fixed and the presentation is variable. This would truly be a reversed paradigm. But there are many human obstacles to getting to this.

So many speak of the need to teach thinking rather than memorizing. In school we learn early not to question things too deeply. We can't open up cabinets to satisfy our curiosity about what's inside. We can't spend time on subjects we want to, rather than what the class is about. And we learn continually that the right answer is the same as everyone else's answer. Even as to current events, we learn to watch and read the mass media and to say the same things as everyone else in the class to appear smart. It's usually a negative factor to ask why something is so. We learn to calculate when 2 canoes will meet on a river, something we'll never need in life, but not one student raises their hand to say that it's not true nor possible. Not one teacher even asks them to think about whether it's true, or ask why it's not true. It's taken as the way to get intelligent.

Computers offer so much opportunity to explore aspects of information creatively. We do teach some of this today, but it's mostly along the lines of learning how to structure a search to get answers. Most often, an outstanding job, better by far, could be done by someone who knows how to program the computer, but we don't consider this a mainstream skill. Even with computers, we expect the answers to just be there for us to pluck.

Hopefully, in the future we will teach the skills of how to manipulate all this placeable information into real problem solutions. The tools on this path will be programming skills, along with multimedia talents. Words can say so much, but the way it's presented to others is what amounts to real communication. These skills should be emphasized in schools of the future. The future?

The future is here today.

Steve Wozniak

Introduction

This book is about change, specifically change that is a result of new technology. Technology has changed how we get information, how we entertain ourselves, how we communicate with others, how we do our work, how we teach, and how we learn. This book is also about why you as an individual and as a teacher must change the way you look at the world.

Most of the time, change is a subtle thing. In fact, change can be downright sneaky. Today, with all the technological development taking place around us, most of us are aware that something has changed in our lives, but it's often very difficult to put our finger on exactly what has happened, how things have changed, or why things are different. It's hard to see because the world is not that different from day to day.

Just think about how our children grow up. We don't see them grow, but they do, right in front of us. It's only when their clothes or shoes don't fit any more, or when we compare them to the photos we took mere weeks or months ago, that we become aware of the magnitude of the changes that are taking place right before our very eyes. It's hard for us to see the change because they're in our face all the time.

Change happens much the same way in the rest of our lives. We don't notice things changing on a daily basis, but when we stop and compare the way things are done now with the way they were done 10 or 20 years ago, we are astonished at the differences. Take how we get information, for example. Today, when you need to find the population of a country or you want to learn about a current world event, you say, "I'll just Google it," and everyone knows what you mean. Ten years ago, Google was in its infancy and had not yet been established in the consciousness of the general public. Twenty years ago, Google didn't even exist.

These are truly amazing times, and change is happening all around us. We live in a world where change has become the constant. As a result, the world as we knew it—even as little as 10 years ago—no longer exists. Hard as it may be to accept, 10 years from now, today's world will have recreated itself many times over. Even if we can acknowledge that the world is changing rapidly, it is almost impossible to quantify and qualify the scope and the scale of the changes we are experiencing.

As a result, many of the personal coping strategies we have learned over the years to deal with change have begun to unravel. They probably began to fail us several years back—we just didn't see that it was happening. If the coping strategies we used a decade ago aren't working well now, it's certain they will be completely useless as we plunge headlong into the 21st century. The only way to survive the impending tempest of change is to learn the art of the chameleon: to recognize when our environment has changed and immediately make changes in our own life so that we continually blend in with the world around us.

This book can help. It contains a number of ideas and strategies that the authors have developed over the course of delivering hundreds of presentations to thousands of educators, administrators, businesses, and professional people throughout North America. We believe that there is a simple formula for adapting to the changes. At the very center of it all, the key issue is our mindset, or paradigm. Paradigm determines how well you handle changes and enables you to recognize and master change in your life. Dealing with change requires us to cultivate a new set of attitudes and skills that are necessary for successfully leveraging the changes for our benefit.

Our journey begins here, because it is our paradigm that most often prevents us from acknowledging change, as well as developing the necessary attitudes and skills needed to deal with it. Once we begin to understand the ways in which our paradigm talks to us (and how it can even paralyze us) we can interpret change from a variety of perspectives. Although the formula for coping with change may be simple, as we will see, adjusting your paradigm can be a considerable challenge.

This book will also analyze a number of key trends that will most certainly affect every aspect of our lives in the 21st century. These trends point to the kind of future we can expect to see very soon. They show us a glimpse of the kind of changes that we will have to make to our paradigm for life and for education if we are going to apply the art of the chameleon. By assessing our paradigms and using our understanding of the way in which the world is changing, we can begin to develop the new skills and strategies that will help us thrive in the 21st century.

Please understand from the outset that the authors do not worship at the altar of technology. We don't suffer from terminal technodrool or technolust. (Well, maybe just a little.) We are educators first and foremost; we are technologists only as a distant second. As a consequence, this book is not about hardware and software, laptops and handheld devices, or even the speed of your Internet connection. Instead, this book is about the change that new technology has created and will continue to create. Technology is now at the heart of most of the change we now experience; the power of new technological tools makes their use compelling. Nevertheless, having access to technology and being able to handle the changes it creates are two fundamentally different issues. We must distinguish between the available technology and the mindset that directs its use.

A Significant Shift in Mindset Has Already Occurred

In the 1990s, we knew we were in the midst of a big change in how the world operated. We just didn't know how big. Now, the picture is much clearer, and what we see is astounding. A significant shift in mindset has occurred in the world since 1995. It is vital that we grasp the importance of what has transpired since then, because a monumental shift has taken place. Although the shift, when it finally happened, took place very quickly, it was a long time coming.

The story began in 1946, when the world's first electronic computer, ENIAC, was turned on and the electronic era began. Despite the importance of this development, electronic technology did not bring about many changes for the average person for almost 50 years. In the late 1970s, the introduction of microcomputers hinted at something big going on. The circle of people who were directly touched by electronic devices grew significantly; however, due to the limited capabilities of microcomputers, the general public was still not affected by these devices in any significant way for many years.

In the late 1980s, laptop computers began appearing. The development of these portable devices meant computing became more visible to the general public. Meanwhile, the increasing power of portable and desktop computers facilitated a shift in the kinds of information that these machines could handle. The ability to process text and graphics made huge leaps forward as the desktop publishing phenomenon swept across the world. By the early 1990s, computers had developed sufficient power to adequately handle photographs, sound, and video. More and more people, companies, and industries were being touched by the growing power of electronic computing.

Then, in 1995, came a pivotal development. A company named Netscape created an easy-to-use piece of software called an Internet browser, and the use of the World Wide Web on the Internet exploded. In his book, *The World Is Flat*, Thomas Friedman claims, "the world has not been the same since" Netscape went public on August 9, 1995 (2005, p. 56). Friedman calls this development one of the forces that flattened the world. It was a gigantic leap forward in what computers could do to affect the lives of average people. It was momentous because three conditions for ubiquitous computer use were finally met:

1. The cost of electronic devices had dropped, allowing the average person to afford them.

2. Computers had increased in power enough to adequately handle a wide range of multimedia information.

3. Individual devices were connected to one another by a global network that facilitated worldwide exchange of that multimedia data.

Why is this so important? Why do we call it a revolution? When the three conditions for ubiquitous computer use were met, technology use quickly became "normal" for the general public. It now had the power to affect everyone and change the way average people lived their lives. It rapidly spawned new ways to communicate with others, new ways to publish information, new ways to collaborate with friends and colleagues, and new ways to learn about areas of interest. As a result, people began to do many things differently.

This is a key point. The change in technology is not as important as the change in the way people acted. In his book, *Here Comes Everybody*, Clay Shirky (2008) comments on the significance of when technology changes what people do: "Revolution doesn't happen when society adopts new technologies—it happens when society adopts new behaviors" (p. 160).

People are doing things differently, and to make that happen they have shifted their mindset from an older view of the way the world operates to a new one—one that is truly suited to the new digital online world of the 21st century.

This is a significant point. This shift has rendered obsolete many aspects of a 20th-century paradigm for how the world operates. In a few short years, everyone who grew up in the 20th century (the vast majority of adults in the world today) has had to quickly adjust their ideas for how things are done to keep up with the unprecedented change that is occurring in the fast-moving world of technologically driven development. Our paradigm is under relentless assault as we are stretched to cope with the speed and breadth of the changes that are cascading into our daily lives. We are experiencing extreme paradigm pressure.

For educators, it is even more challenging because, unlike us, our students have grown up in this new online world. For younger people, those who grew up after 1995, using new digital tools connected to the global network has become transparent. They use these digital tools the way older adults use a pen. For older adults, pens are transparent. We don't marvel at how the pen works or at the significance of its development, we just use it. Most of us don't ever think about the pen when we use it unless it runs out of ink or we can't find it. It's not the pen itself, but what we use the pen for, that concerns us.

That is exactly what it is like for kids using digital technology today. They don't see the tools, they only see the tasks they are trying to accomplish. Young people operate with a different paradigm—one that allows them to use the power of new developments much more quickly and completely than those who are still clinging to their 20th-century paradigm.

This is a huge problem for educators for two reasons. First, kids today increasingly can't relate to many aspects of 20th-century life. The examples and illustrations used by many teachers have little or no meaning for their students. At best, this rapid shift to a new way of doing things has rendered much of our instruction out of touch with the digital culture of our students; at worst, our outdated paradigm is turning kids off. Seemingly overnight, we have a serious engagement problem in our classrooms.

Second, it is our mandate to equip students with knowledge and skills that will make them effective individuals, family members, citizens, and workers in the 21st century. That means we must also project how paradigms will change in the future so we are able to teach students today what they will need for success tomorrow. For these reasons, it is critical that educators embrace a new paradigm for education to keep instruction effective and relevant for 21st-century students.

So what can be done? First, teachers must adapt to a new paradigm for teaching and learning. They must adopt new behaviors for what, where, when, and how they teach students. They must strive to bring their thinking into the 21st century, keeping what is still valid and important while abandoning that which no longer applies. There will be many winners and losers as society moves further into a technology-based world. It is a way of life that we can only begin to imagine. Thus, the key to being a winner in the emerging digital culture of the 21st century is to make a radical shift in our mindset or paradigm for life.

Second, we must look for any clues about what the future will look like. We must identify trends that are occurring today because they can be extrapolated into the future to predict where things are headed. Equipped with this knowledge, we can project the adjustments a person will have to make to their paradigm in order to be successful in the future.

Let's embark on this journey of self-discovery and exploration of the future. It begins with an examination of your paradigm for life and for learning.

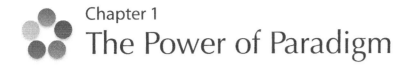

Chapter 1
The Power of Paradigm

> We can't solve problems by using the same kind of thinking we used when we created them.
>
> **Albert Einstein**

What Is a Paradigm?

A paradigm is a frame of reference that helps us make sense out of new information. It is a value system that enables us to determine the significance of events and a filter that interprets those events. Paradigm guides all our actions. It governs everything we do and everything we think. Our paradigm colors our perception of the world and determines how we find meaning in our lives. We use our paradigm to set priorities for our personal and professional lives. It guides us as we pursue success in our relationships, in our work, in our families, in our hobbies, and in our personal entertainment. In his book, *Future Edge*, Joel Barker (1992) defines a paradigm this way:

> *A paradigm is a set of rules and regulations (written and unwritten) that does two things: (1) it establishes or defines boundaries; and (2) it tells you how to be successful inside the boundaries in order to be successful.* (p. 32)

Our paradigm, then, provides us with the rules for how life is to be lived. We develop our paradigm by living in a society that has agreed on certain standards of behavior, on what things are to be valued, on conventions for how things are done. These standards and conventions are so universally accepted within that society that it is assumed this is the only way to live. Common sense and conventional wisdom are dependent on everyone accepting what is common and conventional; they are dependent on people having a shared paradigm.

We acquire most of our paradigm as we pass through our youth. That's when we learn the rules for how to relate to others, what our responsibilities are, and how to succeed in life. So if you want to figure out what your paradigm for life is, then the first place to look is your youth—what life was like as you grew up, what was valued, how things were done, and what behavior was acceptable. It is in your youth when you go to school and acquire your paradigm for teaching and learning as well. The experience you had in school leaves a lasting and powerful impression. In fact, when new teachers stand in front of a class of students for the first time, most teach the way they were taught.

We are usually unaware that we are acquiring a paradigm. It just happens as we function in society. A paradigm consists of theories, dogma, ideas, superstitions, traditions, routines, and habits that we pick up as we live in a family, participate in civic activities, work with people who have done a job longer than we have, and invest personal effort in mastering a certain way of doing things. This last point is particularly important for our discussion because it applies to so much of what we do in education. We have been doing things the same way in our schools for so long that there is a deeply entrenched paradigm for what teaching and learning look like. There is widespread acceptance of what is considered conventional in education. In addition, we have invested so much effort into mastering the rules for success in this paradigm that we have difficulty seeing any other way to do this thing called teaching. That is the insidious thing about a paradigm—it can prevent you from seeing things from another perspective.

In his book, *Powers of the Mind*, Adam Smith says, "When you are in the middle of a paradigm, it is hard to imagine any other paradigm" (1975, p.19). You can't conceive of any other way of doing something because your paradigm confines your thinking to what you know. Your past experience establishes a way of thinking, and you become locked into a certain way of seeing things. The power of paradigm to influence our perception can't be overstated. Here is a simple activity that will help you understand how paradigm can affect perception. Think back to the first time you saw a picture like this:

My Wife and My Mother-In-Law *by cartoonist W. E. Hill, 1915*. Image source: http://commons. wikimedia.org/wiki/File:My_Wife_and_My_Mother-In-Law_(Hill).png

We remember becoming completely frustrated when someone said there were two pictures here: that of an older woman and that of a younger woman. Try as we did, we just couldn't see them both. Then suddenly—and for no apparent reason—our focus shifted and there they both were. Once we understood how to change our focus, it was simple to move back and forth between the two images. In retrospect, it is hard to accept that there was ever a time when we couldn't see both of them. Have you ever had a similar experience?

The point here is that once your mind starts seeing images in a certain way, it takes real effort to see them from a different perspective. In fact, your mindset can actually create perceptual blindness—your mind is so locked into one way of seeing things that it prevents you from seeing something that is staring you in the face. In this example, your mind locks into one image and you can't see the other. You might even call someone crazy if he or she told you there was another woman in the picture once you had already begun to see it in a certain way. It is amazing how your mindset can prevent you from seeing the validity of another viewpoint. And that can be a major problem when something new appears.

What Happens When Something Changes the Rules?

A new development, if it is something significant like computers connected to the online world of digital multimedia information, changes the rules for living. It requires a shift in thinking to keep up with where the world is heading. Barker (1992) terms this a paradigm shift and describes it like this:

> *A paradigm shift, then, is a change to a new game, a new set of rules.* (p. 37)

The real issue when a paradigm shift occurs is how we respond to it. Will we see the real significance of this new development? Will our existing paradigm prevent us from seeing this development from another point of view, a 21st-century point of view? Will we recognize the limits of our current thinking and apply the art of the chameleon to our mindset and invest the time and effort required to shift our paradigm to blend in with the changing world around us? Responding with a willingness to change is very difficult to do because our existing mindset greatly hinders accurate perception.

Here is an example of how the power of paradigm can severely hamper a person's perception of a new development. Imagine the mindset of a farmer in 1908 who relies on horses for transportation. He's in his wagon behind reliable old Bessie, a strong mare with the ability to pull the farmer and his supplies all the way home. On the way to town, both are startled by the sudden appearance of a noisy motorcar, chugging along on its own power. It spooks old Bessie, and it takes considerable effort for the farmer to keep her under control. As the motorcar leaves him choking in its dust, the farmer swears at the folly of this noisy, dirty contraption.

If we were to ask him at that moment whether this automobile would have any significant effect on the future, he wouldn't hesitate to share his perspectives: There's absolutely no future for the automobile, he would tell us. There's not enough gasoline around for these cursed horseless carriages, no one knows how to fix them when they break down, and besides, they scare the horses. Furthermore, there's not enough room on the road for both cars and horses. Building separate roads for motorcars is impractical, so it's a certainty that these blasted things will be gone in a year or two.

From our perspective, as we stand well into the future, it's easy to chuckle at this farmer's shortsightedness. The reality is that the automobile and its spin-off technologies changed everything. In short order, the automobile affected virtually every part of industrialized society. It changed the way we lived, the way we played, and the way we viewed the world. But from where the farmer sat on his wagon behind Bessie, none of this seemed probable or even possible. His mindset, or his paradigm, would not allow him to see change even as it sped by him on the road, blowing dust and fumes in his face. He just couldn't see the future even though it was staring at him.

While we may laugh at him now, it's quite possible for any of us to be in a similar situation as this farmer. It is possible and highly probable for any of us to view a new piece of technology or a new web site and completely miss its true significance. This is because our paradigm is neither ready nor equipped to deal with the new perspective on how things are done that this development represents. Even though the future is staring at us, we just can't see it.

The Lure of the Familiar

The power of paradigm comes from more than its power to influence our perception. It also comes from a person's natural desire for comfort. We tend to become quite comfortable with the way things have always been, and that can be a major obstacle to embracing change. Our desire for comfort can make us cling to what we know when moving to something new is overdue.

One of us has a leather jacket that he bought long ago during the university years. That jacket is a much-loved piece of clothing. Despite its dilapidated condition, he still wears that jacket today, some 20-plus years later, any time the opportunity arises. It has rips and stains, it's out of style, and it doesn't fit the way it used to. So what? When people comment about how shabby it is, he just tells them that it's not old, it has character! Sadly, others don't share this perspective. In fact, the condition of the jacket has deteriorated to the point where his wife has warned him that if he ever leaves their house again wearing it, she will personally incinerate it, quite possibly with him in it!

Yet, despite all of these dire threats, he just can't bring himself to get rid of it or buy another one. Why? Because that old jacket is just so darn comfortable. Besides, it took so long to break it in, that the thought of going through that process again with a new coat is too unsettling. He would rather put up with the incredulous looks than buy a new one. The problem is that it took a lot of hard work to make that jacket comfortable. He knows that he can afford to buy a new one, but he doesn't want to. If he bought a new one, he'd have to start all over again from scratch. Getting comfortable with it would take time. Consequently, he's reluctant (some might suggest resistant) to making what his wife and friends believe is an absolutely necessary change.

Most people have items somewhere in their lives that have become so comfortable they just can't seem to part with them. For most of us, these are special items that have personal meaning. It's human nature to cling to what is familiar and comfortable. Change is consistently resisted because it represents work and is often a threat to our comfort level.

Paradigm Paralysis

There would be no sense in belaboring the point that an established paradigm and a desire for comfort have great power if all we were talking about was their power to make people hold on to old coats and chairs. But an established paradigm and a desire for comfort can have much more significant effects on people. People can become attached to ideas, certain ways of doing things, even views of the world. These mental patterns become like an old coat; they make no great demands upon us, and because we are used to them, we hold on to them for too long. Once we have invested the initial effort in making an idea our own, it's very easy to avoid dealing with changes that may force us to embrace new or different ways of thinking. Consider the difficulty people had in accepting that the world was round or that the earth revolved around the sun.

Let's examine a real example of how an established paradigm and a desire for comfort combined to create perceptual blindness in people in the watchmaking industry. It is the story of the invention of the digital watch. In his book, *Paradigms: The Business of Discovering the Future* (1993), Joel Barker details this remarkable story. Before the digital watch was invented, there was a paradigm for watches. It was an analog device that included gears, springs, levers, jewels, and the need for winding daily. Time was displayed by continuously moving hands. At that time, most of the world's watches were produced in Switzerland. In 1970, the Swiss controlled 85 percent of the world's production of fine watches. Watches and clocks had looked and worked the same way for literally hundreds of years, and this was a firmly established mindset. It was this paradigm that nearly killed the Swiss watchmaking industry.

When the first digital watch was developed by Swiss scientists in the early 1970s, the response from the Swiss watchmaking industry was fascinating. They carefully considered this new device and noted that it didn't have gears, springs, moving parts, jewels, or a need to be wound. Applying their existing paradigm, they dismissed the digital watch by concluding that it really wasn't a watch. Seeing little value in this new product, they subsequently sold it to Texas Instruments. In turn, Texas Instruments sold it to Seiko. It was not the Swiss, but their Japanese competitors, who saw the market potential for the digital watch. It was the Japanese who brought the digital watch to the world in the mid-1970s, and it was the Japanese who quickly took the world market for watches away from the Swiss. As a result, by 1980, the Japanese produced 33 percent of the world's watches and controlled more than 65 percent of the profits from the manufacture of watches. Meanwhile, the Swiss were left holding less than 10 percent of the market. More than 50,000 of 62,000 Swiss watchmakers lost their jobs in less than two years as a direct result of this oversight. Even though their very own researchers had created the new paradigm, Swiss watchmakers missed its potential because of their mindset.

This is paradigm paralysis. It happens when your past experience combines with your desire for comfort to prevent you from seeing things from a different perspective. Paradigm paralysis can even make you blind to the reality that is right in front of your eyes. The story of these Swiss watchmakers shows what can happen to people's ability to see the true meaning of something new when they are caught in paradigm paralysis. We are no longer talking about old coats and chairs. We are talking about devastating effects on the lives of people trying to make a living. The results of paradigm paralysis can be swift and catastrophic for those who are held in its grip.

Keep in mind that the new devices were a radical departure from what watches had looked like for a long time. Some simply dismissed the new devices as toys that would have little or no real effect on the industry. Besides, how could they possibly approach the quality and accuracy of fine Swiss watches? Because they were such a radical departure from what had been, it was hard to even consider them real watches.

By relying on their old paradigms, the Swiss were blind to the true power of the new electronic watch, and so they ignored it. This was a critical mistake. Within a few short years, the global watch market shifted as sales of electronic digital watches overtook and then left behind old-fashioned, gear-based analog watches. Swiss watchmakers hardly knew what had hit them. They were unable to compete because their response was significantly compromised by their paradigm.

This is an important story for educators to consider because there are so many parallels to what is happening in education today. Like the Swiss with their well-established ideas about watches, educators hold a long-standing, established paradigm for what teaching and learning look like.

Technology has created new ways of doing many of the things that teachers and students have traditionally done: new ways for teachers to communicate with students and new ways for students to communicate with each other; new instant access to online multimedia information that can be used in discussions, essays, reports, labs, and so on; new ways to search for information; new ways for students to publish their work including videos, web sites, blogs, wikis, desktop publishing, sound recordings, mashups, and interactive multimedia; and new tools for doing all these things including laptops, smartphones, iPods, iPhones, iPads, or multimedia headsets. The question for teachers is, how are we going to respond to these new developments in the field of education?

Unfortunately, up to this point, educators have looked at these new developments and dismissed them, concluding that they have no real place in the classroom because they don't fit the existing mindset for how instruction takes place. As a result, we face a serious crisis in education because teachers (and administrators, school district staff, school board members, and politicians) have not adjusted their paradigm for teaching and learning to keep pace with the digital world that their students experience every day. Almost everyone involved in education today is caught in paradigm paralysis.

Paradigm Paralysis in the Classroom

We aren't the first educators to be caught in paradigm paralysis. Dealing with the changes brought by new technology has been a challenge that teachers have had to face for hundreds of years, and each new development put pressure on the existing paradigm to adapt. Here are some paraphrased examples of paradigm paralysis in the classroom as researched by Father Stanley Bezuska of Boston College, as told in David Thornburg's book, *Edutrends 2010: Restructuring, Technology, and the Future of Education* (1992, pp. 58–59):

- At a teacher's conference in 1703, it was reported that students could no longer prepare bark to calculate problems. They depended instead on expensive slates. There was great concern over what students would do when the slate was dropped and broken.

- In 1815, it was reported at a principal's meeting that students depended too much on paper. They no longer knew how to write on a slate without getting dust all over themselves. What would happen when they ran out of paper?

- The National Association of Teachers reported in 1907 that students depended too much on ink and no longer knew how to use a knife to sharpen a pencil.

- According to the *Rural American Teacher* in 1928, students depended too much on store-bought ink. They did not know how to make their own. What would happen when they ran out? They would not be able to write until their next trip to the settlement.

- In 1950, it was observed that ballpoint pens would be the ruin of education. Students were using these devices and then throwing them away. The values of thrift and frugality were being discarded. Businesses and banks would never allow such expensive luxuries, according to the educators of the time.

In retrospect, it's easy to see that these teachers were as shortsighted as the Swiss watchmakers. Although these were not stupid individuals, they kept tripping over their paradigms. Their perception of the impact of new technology was greatly affected by their established view of the world. They had no context for the innovations they were contemplating. Embracing the new would have required them to let go of ideas and experience gained before they had this new technology. They would have to leave behind the mindset they had acquired through hard work and a significant investment of time learning to do things the old way. Letting go of the past is one of the most difficult and uncomfortable aspects of dealing with change.

The Need for Paradigm Pliability

Some may say, "Okay, so people have struggled with new inventions in the past. Sure, the farmer on his wagon couldn't see the potential of the automobile at first, but he would likely have ended up using a tractor to plow his fields and a truck to haul his crops before he retired. Those Swiss watchmakers finally caught on and are back in the game. Yes, educators have had to face new technologies throughout history and have been caught in paradigm paralysis as a result. The use of the ballpoint pen was resisted at first because teachers couldn't see its true potential thanks to their previous paradigm for writing utensils, but teachers recovered from this perceptual blindness and eventually embraced the pen as an effective tool for learning. In fact, for many of the people reading this book, the ballpoint pen was an indispensable tool when they were in school. So why all the concern over paradigm paralysis in education? Just like Swiss watchmakers, teachers will catch on in the long run and make the necessary adjustments to embrace new developments. What is so different about the changes we are facing?"

There are two main differences between the change brought by the development of the ballpoint pen and the change we face today from the dawn of the digital world. First, as we will discuss later in this book, the technology available is exceedingly more powerful than anything we have ever seen before in human history. Second, we have much less time to shift to a new paradigm. The shift to the widespread use of the automobile took many years to transpire. The transition to the widespread use of the ballpoint pen was similar; it took place gradually. However, we are seeing more significant paradigm shifts occur much more quickly. In his book, *The Singularity Is Near*, Ray Kurzweil (2005) comments on the difference in the speed of change in the past compared to the speed of change today:

> *A half millennium ago, the product of a paradigm shift such as the printing press took about a century to be widely deployed. Today, the products of major paradigm shifts, such as cellphones and the World Wide Web, are widely adopted in only a few years' time.* (p. 42)

We can't escape the technology changes that are occurring worldwide. Yet these changes are giving us less and less time to adjust to new ways of doing things. This press of time exacerbates the problem of paradigm paralysis, making those caught in its grip vulnerable to being hopelessly out of step with the world in a very short time. We do not have the luxury of sufficient time to wait for teachers to get used to using Google and YouTube. And even if we did wait for that to happen, in our rapidly changing world, by the time the teachers were used to those tools, they would be superseded by newer tools that are many times more powerful. No, in the modern world, we can't allow teachers to linger in paradigm paralysis.

So we must find a new way of thinking that will empower educators. We must set a goal of acquiring paradigm pliability. Paradigm pliability is a mindset that, in times of change, recognizes the limitations of an existing paradigm, adjusts or abandons part of that paradigm, and embraces new ways of doing things to keep pace with a changing environment. Acquiring paradigm pliability is the key to learning the art of the chameleon.

Learning From the Experience of Those Who Have Gone Before Us

Before we leave our discussion of the Swiss watchmakers, there's something else you should know. The desperation in the Swiss watchmaking industry after the sudden emergence of digital watches led Swiss companies to take drastic steps to avoid the complete collapse of their businesses. Swatch Group—as in Swiss (Made) Watch—launched their product line worldwide in 1983. They offered watches in bold, colorful designs. Because of the variety of colors and fun designs, it was not uncommon for someone to wear more than one Swatch at a time, as part of his or her clothing (Pop Swatch), or as a hair accessory. They were reasonably priced for a Swiss-made watch and became wildly popular as fashion collectibles. In addition to offering versatility and creative designs, the Swiss found ways to reduce the number of components from 91 to 51 without the loss of accuracy.

Swatch Group, the world's largest watchmaker, projects that revenue for 2010 will exceed $5.68 billion. They adopted a pliable mindset in order to compete in the new business environment and have been successful.

Reading about how teachers struggled with new technology in the past, it is clear that their dismissal of something new was shortsighted and counterproductive to teaching their students about the world they would enter upon graduation. We must strive not to make the same mistake now. When teachers look at the technological developments of today—which are incredibly more powerful than anything educators have ever faced before—we must apply what we have learned from these stories to escape the grip of paradigm paralysis. We must learn from the Swiss and what they did in their desperation after the collapse of the analog watchmaking industry.

There is hope for those suffering from paradigm paralysis. We can change our paradigm and acquire paradigm pliability. That's good news for educators because we face a more difficult challenge than most. We must not only catch up with new paradigms, but we must also look into the future and project how paradigms will change again so we can better prepare our students for success in that world. But there's a catch—we have to be willing to take drastic measures to make it happen. The theme of this book is that by paying attention to the trends that are occurring in the world today, by stepping back from our existing paradigms of life, and by learning to let go of our old mindsets for teaching and learning, we can learn to embrace and leverage change without being left behind.

Summarizing the Main Points

- A paradigm is a value system that guides all our actions.

- Being in the middle of one paradigm makes it very difficult to see things from another perspective.

- The true issue is how we respond to a paradigm shift.

- Our desire for comfort can make us cling to what we know when moving to something new is overdue.

- Change is consistently resisted because it represents work and is often a threat to our comfort level.

- Paradigm paralysis can make you blind to the reality that is right in front of your eyes. The result can be swift and catastrophic for those who are held in its grip.

- We face a serious crisis in education because educators have not adjusted their paradigm for teaching and learning to keep pace with the digital world that their students experience every day.

- We now have much less time to shift to a new paradigm, and we are seeing more significant paradigm shifts occur much more quickly.

- Paradigm pliability is a mindset that, in times of change, recognizes the limitations of an existing paradigm; adjusts or abandons part of that paradigm; and embraces new ways of doing things to keep pace with a changing environment.

Some Questions to Consider

- Based on what you have read, what do you understand now that you didn't understand before, and why is it important?

- What is "paradigm paralysis," and why is it harmful to education in our new digital age?

- How do we achieve paradigm pliability in the age of exponential change and constant technological innovation? How about in schools?

- What are some of the learning paradigms, or sets of established rules, that were in place in schools 10 or 20 years ago, but are no longer applicable today?

- Why is there so much change while, at the same time, a continued call for change seems to be a constant theme?

Chapter 2
Assessing Your Paradigm

> The art of progress is to preserve order amid change, and to preserve change amid order.
>
> **Alfred North Whitehead**

This book is about the changes that lie ahead. Before we can appreciate the implications of the great changes taking place now and those that will surely occur in the future, we must understand how our past has shaped our view of the world. Remember that the key to the future is people, not technology. The key attribute of successful people in the future will be their paradigm for life. It's important for each of us to identify the paradigm that shapes our perceptions.

How do you understand one's paradigm? How can you identify what experiences or perspectives color a person's thoughts? In this exercise, we are not trying to get a comprehensive picture of all aspects of how our thoughts are formed. Instead, we're focusing on the amount of change that we experienced in our youth and the role technology has played in our lives. To do this, we must look at when and how our younger years relate to the explosion of online digital tools.

Take a few minutes to answer the following true or false questions. Answer honestly and remember that the questions relate to when you were growing up (before you reached the age of 20).

1. I remember when bubble gum cost a penny.
2. I remember when world events were things you read about.
3. I grew up without using a microwave oven.
4. Our household telephone had a rotary dial and no answering machine.
5. I remember when encyclopedias were only printed on paper.
6. I washed dirty dishes by hand.
7. I have no videotapes of my youth.
8. My father or mother worked for one company for 20 years or more.
9. Growing up, I expected to have one career in my life.
10. I printed my emails.
11. I remember getting an Atari for my birthday.
12. I used a computer that did not have a mouse.
13. I used a computer that had either 5¼-inch or 3½-inch floppy disks and no Internet connection.
14. I listened to music on 33 rpm or 45 rpm records or cassette tapes.
15. I communicated online with friends and family by email.

Analyzing Your Score

If three or fewer of the statements in this paradigm quiz describe your life experience before you reached the age of 20, then you probably experienced a technology-rich environment as you grew up, where change was an ever-present factor to be dealt with. The changes taking place in life today are not likely to be causing you a great deal of mental anguish. Read on; just because you are having less trouble with the changes we are experiencing now does not mean you are exempt from the effects of change that will happen in the future.

If four to six of these statements describe your youth, then your youth likely began before the new age of technology, but extended into it. You've also experienced a relatively technology-rich environment, and you know the effects of increasing change as a common part of life. However, you will probably have more difficulty adapting to change than those who experienced this environment all their lives.

If seven or more of these statements describe your life experience before you reached the age of 20, then you probably grew up before microelectronic technology exploded into our lives. We expect the majority of readers of this book to fall into this category. Your experience in life today stems directly from your past. Your youth did not prepare you for a world of constant change and the increasing use of powerful technologies. It's important to understand the implications of the world that shaped your mindset if you want to prepare for success in the radical new world emerging as we enter the 21st century.

It's Not Just the Older Generation

Examining the worldviews described in this paradigm quiz, we begin to understand that everyone has a paradigm. We also begin to see that all of us, even the youngest, must do some unlearning. Whether we are 6, 12, or 18 years old or older, we all have a set picture of the way we think life should unfold. To skillfully change our paradigms and cultivate the ability to embrace change, we must learn to let go of our old paradigms.

If you grew up before the age of high technology, you were prepared for life in the Industrial Age society. You expected to live in much the same way your parents and grandparents lived, with ideas and institutions that have existed for hundreds of years. This once-successful approach to life is deeply entrenched in the public consciousness. Some changes and adjustments have happened slowly over time in the industrial society, but the basic premise for living has not changed significantly. This is likely the experience of many people reading this book, so it is important that we take a moment to examine the basic foundations of life in the late Industrial Age.

The Major Foundations of Industrial Life

The Industrial Age can be described as the age of mass production. This era began 300 years ago with the automation of industrial equipment using steam power. The idea of production on a massive scale was refined when Adam Smith developed the idea of the division of labor. This concept was further refined early in the 20th century by Eli Whitney, Henry Ford, and

Frederick Winslow Taylor. Taylor captured the essence of this new approach to production in his book, *The Principles of Scientific Management* (1911). His principles were used to build modern production facilities that created an assembly line. These developments allowed the production of goods at an unprecedented rate. The mass production of goods had profound and immediate effects on business, education, and people.

Mass production resulted in a society based on standardization. The assembly line approach to production did not allow for much, if any, customization. There was a remarkable cookie-cutter mentality to business, education, and even personal life. Society stamped out a look and feel for life that was almost identical for all. Often, the needs and desires of the individual were sacrificed in favor of the perceived average needs and desires of the masses. When asked about custom paint jobs on his cars, Henry Ford once replied, "You can have any color as long as it's black."

This cookie-cutter mindset persists widely today. How often have you gone into a shop wanting to make changes to a product or service being offered, only to be told that it's impossible, will take a long time, or will be very expensive? As a result of that mindset, we are TTWWADIed (That's the Way We've Always Done It) to death. In fact, the attitude of many people in business is "take it or leave it," which has its roots in the Industrial Age paradigm. In this paradigm, those who manufactured items decided what the people wanted and what they needed.

Industrial life also led to the age of the specialist. In the assembly line, people specialized in a particular part of the production process and focused only on their job, not concerning themselves with the things that happened before or after their particular task. Specialization often meant that individual workers did not have a sense of the whole process. It also meant that people, in order to be successful, needed the ability to blindly follow instructions. It was a basic foundation for all of industrial life, extending far beyond the production line. Have you ever asked a person in a bank, department store, or insurance company for assistance only to be told, "That's not my department!" This kind of specialization and compartmentalization is typical of Industrial Age thinking.

Business in the industrial world involved central planning, control from the top down, and a hierarchical structure of management. People working in industrial companies climbed the ladder to success, moving up the organization's hierarchy of management one step at a time. Large amounts of money were needed to build production facilities, so the Industrial Age gave rise to the large corporation. These companies were large enough to have the resources needed to produce, sell, and distribute many items to large markets. These large companies were also able to provide benefits to their employees that had never before been offered. By the latter half of the 20th century, employees enjoyed pensions, medical plans, and other benefits that were a direct result of the success of this model.

Industrial life was also amazingly predictable. The assembly lines created by large companies made for lives that were filled with the repetition of making similar products day in and day out. Life followed the same pattern year after year. Frequently, people would be employed by a single company for their entire working career; however, job satisfaction was typically low. Because of the division of labor and the specialization of tasks, an individual felt like nothing more than a small cog in a huge process that was completely out of his or her control. Many times, individuals never understood the whole process of production that they were involved in for their entire careers.

If you grew up in this society, its paradigm has been imprinted on your subconscious mind. Increasingly, this mindset is out of sync with the world in which we now live. People continue to operate from the assumption that little, if anything, has changed. They continue to think the old ways of doing things still work and are having an increasingly difficult time functioning. When confronted with change in their lives and in their world, they experience conflict and upheaval. This leads to an increased yearning for life to return to the way it used to be. This is a good news/bad news scenario. The good news is that they know something is happening. That something is the Information Age. The bad news is that there will be more struggle and discomfort if they persist in trying to make an Industrial Age paradigm work in the Information Age. What we need is a new mindset that can leverage the power of the technological change.

Now Let's Assess Your Paradigm for Teaching and Learning

A major focus of this book is changing education to match the realities of 21st-century life. Understanding your paradigm for life prepares you for the adjustments you must make to keep up with our changing world. If you are a teacher, you must also understand your paradigm for teaching and learning. You will have to change your ideas about education to ensure that your students can keep up with our changing world as well.

Take a few minutes to answer the following true or false questions. Answer honestly and remember that the questions relate to when you were growing up (before you reached the age of 20).

1. In my classes, the teacher talked and the students listened. Students were not allowed to talk in class unless they raised their hand.

2. When a bell rang, students moved to a new class.

3. I received black-and-white photocopied learning materials.

4. Research was a physical act: You walked to the library and searched the stacks.

5. I copied sections out of a paper-based encyclopedia for my schoolwork.

6. I took multiple-choice tests.

7. My teachers taught theory without its application to life.

8. My teachers were the experts in the classroom.

9. I wrote essays or lab reports by hand with a pen.

10. The goal was to get good grades, not necessarily to learn new skills.

11. I answered questions correctly on tests without really knowing what the answers meant. The emphasis was on memorizing facts instead of forming opinions.

12. A teacher became impatient or disciplined a student if he or she started asking questions about the material in a class. No matter what my teacher said, what mattered in class was what was on the tests.

13. The teacher taught a lesson, and then students answered questions from the board or from the end of a chapter in the textbook.

14. The only technology used in the classroom was an overhead projector.

15. Good grades in school meant a good job when you graduated.

Analyzing Your Score

If three or fewer of the statements in this second paradigm quiz describe your school experience before you reached the age of 20, then you probably experienced a technology-rich, 21st-century instructional environment as you grew up. You are better equipped to handle the changes taking place today than just about everyone else involved in education. Again, read on, because you are not exempt from feeling pressure from new developments.

If four to six of these statements describe your experience in school, then at least some of your time as a student was spent in a classroom where the teaching and learning was modeled on 20th-century Industrial Age ideas for education. Your thinking about teaching has been partially influenced by outdated ideas.

If seven or more of these statements describe your school experience before you reached the age of 20, then you definitely attended a school based on 20th-century thinking, regardless of when you graduated. Again, we expect the majority of readers of this book to fall into this category. Your ideas about teaching and learning stem directly from your experience as a student in a school that was designed for a different world than the one we live in today.

Old Ideas About Teaching and Learning

It is important to examine the origins of our current school system because, for almost all of us, our ideas about teaching and learning have been greatly influenced by the thinking that underlies the way our schools operate. This is a critical step in implementing change in education. We must identify the major aspects of the thinking that exists in the minds of educators if we hope to change our paradigm for success in the future.

The basic organization of our current schools and the school day dates back to the early 1900s when the world was excited about the success of Henry Ford's assembly line. With such dramatic improvements in productivity at the Ford Motor Company, there was great excitement about applying that kind of thinking widely across society. Schools were not exempt. According to Linda Darling-Hammond in her 1997 book, *The Right to Learn*, William Wirt came up with the idea of the "platoon school" in 1908.

Hoping to save on wasted plant space and solve overcrowding in schools, Wirt devised a system in which students circulate through the school from one classroom to another, with different teachers teaching them different subjects, and for shorter periods of time (Darling-Hammond, 1997, p. 41).

Under this system, schools were modeled after the assembly line and teachers specialized in only one subject, teaching it repeatedly throughout the day. Teachers abandoned the holistic approach in which they had taught many subjects to a wide range of ages. They began teaching a single subject to students who were all the same age. Schools were organized into departments to further the specialization of teachers. Teachers were given classrooms in which they would teach for short periods of time, usually an hour. A bell would ring and the students would move from one specialist to another. The basic layout of today's high school, with its hallways, classrooms, and departments, was created before the Great Depression.

Also in the early years of the 20th century, decisions about teaching, curriculum, assessment, and learning passed from the hands of teachers to administrators, commercial textbook publishers, and test makers who were not concerned with the needs of individual students. Instructional standards were introduced into education at this time as well. These standards were to be used with extensive tests so the teacher could know at all times whether instruction was progressing as it should.

As early as 1926, behaviorist theories were put into practice in schools. B. F. Skinner further modified this thinking in 1954. The behaviorist approach to learning asserted that giving students only small, discrete portions of information in a predetermined sequence would improve performance. The key to this approach was immediate positive reinforcement for correct short responses that had been learned by rote. This approach reinforced the kind of memorization skills that were critical for life on the production lines of the Industrial Age. It was rapidly adopted in schools, and while subsequent research in cognitive psychology has identified considerable limitations to behaviorist theory, this approach to learning persists to the present.

A Problem for Teachers

The power of this long-established paradigm for what schools do has touched almost everyone in our society. Even if you grew up in the technology-rich, online world, you probably went to a school based on outdated 20th-century Industrial Age ideas about what teaching and learning look like. We have watched in amazement as young teachers who have just graduated from teacher training start out their careers teaching just like teachers did 50 years ago. The established ideas about what teachers and students are supposed to do are so pervasive it is almost impossible to escape their influence. Because the thinking behind our current instructional approach was developed so long ago, nothing in our educational paradigm has equipped teachers to deal with the digital world.

We face the prospect that critical decisions in education are being made by people who do not really understand the full implications of the changes taking place in the world, especially the world of kids. Without this knowledge, they do not understand the effect these changes might have on the decisions they are making. This includes not only the teacher in the classroom, but parents, school administrators, school district staff, school board members, and local, state, provincial, and national politicians. These decision makers are resisting change because old ideas shape their worldview and change could bring unwelcome struggle.

Making Changes From the Inside Out

There are many who believe that the high schools of today are radically different from the schools of the early 20th century. They point to having computers, networking, air- conditioning, skylights, video surveillance, telephones in classrooms, digital phone and PA systems, sophisticated digital whiteboards in classrooms, and a multitude of other improvements as proof that schools have changed. However, the underlying organization of the school and the basic instructional approach have remained the same for nearly a century. Teachers still talk to students as they sit passively in their seats (at least, until a bell rings). This and many other established paradigms continue to be the main teaching strategies for a vast majority of educators.

Summarizing the Main Points

- To skillfully change our paradigms and cultivate the ability to embrace change, we must learn to let go of our old paradigms.

- The Industrial Age can be described as the age of mass production.

- The mass production of goods had profound and immediate effects on business, education, and people. Mass production resulted in a society based on standardization.

- There will be more struggle and discomfort if we persist in trying to make an Industrial Age paradigm work in the Information Age. What we need is a new mindset that can leverage the power of the technological change.

- Understanding your paradigm for life prepares you for the adjustments you must make to keep up with our changing world. If you are a teacher, you must also understand your paradigm for teaching and learning.

- We must identify the major aspects of the thinking that exists in the minds of educators if we hope to change our paradigm for success in the future.

- The basic layout of today's high school was created before the Great Depression.

- Because the thinking behind our current instructional approach was developed so long ago, nothing in our educational paradigm has equipped teachers to deal with the digital world.

Some Questions to Consider

- Why is there so much change, yet a continued call for change seems to be a constant theme?

- Based on what you have read, what do you understand now that you didn't understand before, and why is it important?

- Based on what you have just read, brainstorm on the topic of what it will mean to be educated in the 21st century.

- Why change in the first place? What are your current systems/structures, and how can they be improved?

- Does the change process ever end? If not, what are some ways to keep it under control?

Chapter 3
Checkmate!

> With 30 linear steps, you get to 30.
> With 30 steps exponentially, you get to one billion.
>
> **Ray Kurzweil**

The world has changed radically since 1995. Consequently, most adults are experiencing paradigm pressure. The paradigm that served them so well in the past has very quickly become ill-suited to the online digital reality of the world today.

For people born before 1970, today's world can be a bewildering place. They did not use computers when they were in high school. They did not enroll in Preparations for the Online Digital World 101 while in college. Their worldview, their understanding of society, and their perspectives on the structure of things were formed from an industrial model of thinking.

They did not anticipate that they would need to know how to integrate "smart" electronic devices into their lives or receive and interpret new kinds of visual information. No one could foresee the implications of instantaneous global communication. For many, technology has so radically altered the way life is lived that they stay away from the online digital world as often as possible, avoiding it completely in many cases. They are not equipped to deal with the world now unfolding before them.

For people born between 1970 and 1985, the world is only slightly less baffling. They did not have instantaneous and global access to the online world in their youth. While they did use computers in high school for computer programming, word processing, desktop publishing, database applications, and email, they did not grow up with cell phones, text messages, online social networking, massive multiplayer online role-playing games, instant messaging, mashups, or sites with a worldwide reach like those of Twitter, Facebook, Wikipedia, Amazon, eBay, or craigslist. Although these people are more comfortable with technology, they are being pressed by the new online reality.

For those born after 1985, the online digital world is a comfortable place. They are much more at ease with the way the world operates than those who are older. But if they become teachers, they can't escape the imprint of the old thinking that underlies our school system.

They may be able to use Facebook to connect with their friends, but they have almost no model for how to use it as a positive teaching tool. Like their older colleagues, they experience paradigm pressure when it comes to shifting their instructional approach to reflect the realities of the modern world.

Make no mistake about it: The speed of change is increasing. But how much will technology really increase in power? How different will the world be in the future? We can get a pretty accurate picture of the future if we understand a fundamental truth about the nature of technology: It develops exponentially faster over time.

Ray Kurzweil (2005) discusses this idea in his book, *The Singularity Is Near*. When researching his book, he consulted with a number of experts in technological development, as well as a number of respected reference works, to get a picture of what has happened to the speed of change over time. He discovered this:

> . . . *an unmistakable exponential trend: key events have been occurring at an ever-hastening pace.* (Kurzweil, p. 26)

The key words here are *exponential trend*. Trends start in the past and help us to understand why things are the way they are in the present. More importantly, trends can be extrapolated into the future to give us an idea of where things are heading. The trend identified by Kurzweil deserves very close attention. What does "exponential trend" mean, and what implications does it have for our discussion of mounting paradigm pressure? Let's first explore the meaning of this word *exponential*.

Exponential is a mathematical term referring to a number raised to a certain power. For example, the expression 2^3 represents the number that results when 2 is raised to the third power: $2 \times 2 \times 2 = 8$. The number 3 in this expression is called the exponent. Exponential expressions can represent very large numbers. Exponential growth in a trend means that as time passes, the trend increases in its influence at an ever more astounding rate. It is critical that we grasp what kind of growth we can expect when trends are exponential in nature.

Here is a story that can help us understand the power of exponential growth. It is an old fable from the Middle East of a peasant farmer who saves his king from a tiger attack. The king was so grateful that he offered to give the farmer anything he desired, up to half of the kingdom. The farmer responded this way: "Oh my king, I am a simple man and your humble servant. Grant me only this one simple request."

Taking a chessboard in his hand, the farmer went on. "All I ask is that you give me one kernel of wheat in the first square of this board. Then, each day, fill the next square with double the number of kernels until each square of the board is filled." The king was impressed with this peasant. He had not asked for gold or jewels as the king had expected. So the king agreed to the farmer's seemingly modest request.

Before you read any further, guess how much the king will have to give this peasant by the time the deal is done. (There are 64 squares on a chessboard.) Now, let's see how modest the farmer's request really was. Here are the numbers of wheat kernels that would fill each square of the chessboard.

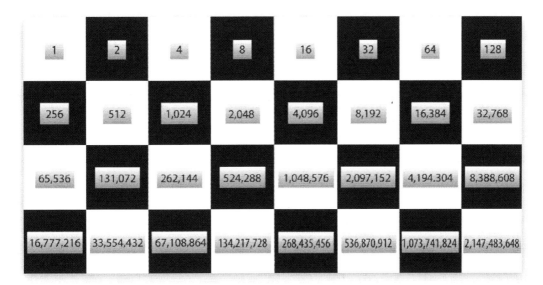

We are halfway through the farmer's request and the king has to put a little over two billion kernels of wheat in the 32nd square. That sounds like a lot, but how much wheat is this really? According to the Yahoo! Answers web site (www.answers.yahoo.com), there are approximately 10,000–18,000 kernels of wheat in a pound, or an average of 14,000 kernels per pound.

According to the Kansas State University Research web site (www.oznet.ksu.edu/aawf/June_26.htm), a modern railcar can hold 240,000 pounds of wheat. That translates to 3,360,000,000 kernels of wheat in a modern railcar if there are 14,000 kernels per pound of wheat.

At the halfway point in the farmer's request, the king is putting enough wheat in a square to fill two-thirds of a railcar. Although the doubling of the number of kernels has begun to make the farmer richer than he has ever been in his life, it is still of little concern to the king with his vast storehouses of grain. But let's see where things go from here.

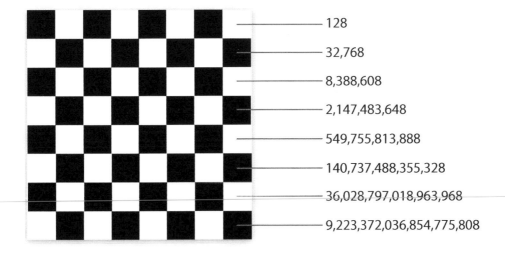

This is an astonishingly large number! In Square 64 the king must put in roughly 9.2 quintillion kernels of wheat! The number is represented mathematically as 2^{64}. When all the squares are added together, we see that the king is on the hook for roughly 18.4 quintillion kernels—that's 18,400 quadrillion or 18,400,000 trillion! How can we grasp such an enormous number? The total number of kernels of wheat the king would have to give the farmer would fill roughly 5.6 billion modern railcars. The entire world could not produce that amount of grain! The farmer obviously knew more about exponential growth than the king.

The point of this story is that whenever you are dealing with any trend that is exponential—look out! The growth in the power of the trend to influence your life may start slowly just like the growth in the number of kernels of wheat the farmer received in the first few squares of this chessboard; but when the trend begins to pick up speed, the influence will overwhelm you in very short order, just as the number of kernels given the farmer exploded into astronomically high numbers before the squares on the chessboard were filled. If you ever encounter the word *exponential* when looking at trends, be sure to take notice!

There are two important aspects of exponential growth in the story of the farmer and the king worth noting. First, it takes a while before the doubling has much effect on the number of kernels of wheat. This delay in impact is why many miss the significance of new trends that appear in technological development. New areas of technology may appear to be very limited in power, or even silly, at first and are given little attention or ignored altogether. This is what happened when the World Wide Web first appeared. Bill Gates gave an address at the Comdex Trade Show in Las Vegas in 1994 in which he said, "I see no commercial potential for the World Wide Web for at least 10 years" (Gates, Comdex, 1994). Businesses began making money on the World Wide Web almost immediately after Gates's speech, and by the year 2004, it was generating billions of dollars of revenue annually. Why couldn't Gates see it when he made his speech? In 1994, the exponential development was in its infancy and so the explosive nature of its future growth was difficult to detect.

Second, once the exponential growth really kicks in, the increase in power is quickly overwhelming. When you are dealing with things that are developing exponentially, you cannot deal with only what is occurring each day—you will quickly be buried in wheat! As time progresses, you will have less time to deal with more growth. The only way to handle exponential change is to anticipate what will happen tomorrow.

In the story of the farmer and the king, the trend doubled in power. Can you imagine how much wheat the farmer would receive if he had asked the king to triple the number of kernels for each new square (3^{64})? The numbers would be so incredibly high it would be almost impossible to comprehend. What if they quadrupled in each square (4^{64})? Or quintupled (5^{64})? The growth would be so overwhelming so quickly the king wouldn't know what hit him. And that's the point. If you are not thinking ahead in times of exponential change, then you won't know what hit you.

If technological development is an exponential trend, no wonder we are experiencing paradigm pressure. The increase in the power of each new tool is significantly more than the one that preceded it. It is mounting a continual assault on our industrial-style thinking. If we are to have any hope of escaping from the paradigm pressure we are all experiencing, then we must shift our thinking and focus on the future.

Summarizing the Main Points

- Most adults are experiencing paradigm pressure. The paradigm that served them so well in the past has very quickly become ill-suited to the online digital reality of the world today.

- We can get an accurate picture of the future if we understand a fundamental truth about the nature of technology: It develops exponentially faster over time.

- Exponential growth in a trend means that as time passes, the trend increases in its influence at an ever more astounding rate.

- If you are not thinking ahead in times of exponential change, then you won't know what hit you.

Some Questions to Consider

- Based on what you have read, what do you understand now that you didn't understand before, and why is it important?

- What have you done to anticipate the future and to identify the new experiences you're going to discover that will be driven by technology change?

- What technologies do you use today that you didn't have 20 years ago? How many of them can you bring to school with you?

- Does the change process ever end? What are some of the ways that you can keep it under control?

Chapter 4
Living Life Like a Quarterback

> We would accomplish many more things if we didn't think of them as impossible.
>
> **Vince Lombardi**

How do we deal with a world where things are changing exponentially? Unlike kids who have grown up in a world of accelerated change, adults can remember a time when change was slower and more manageable. For these people, today's fast-paced world with its whirlwind of technologically driven exponential change presents them with an uncomfortable environment for which they are unprepared. Things haven't just changed, they continue to change—development after development cascades into everyday life, overwhelming their ability to handle difficult situations. Modern life is disquieting at best and absolutely bewildering at worst. Although some of the older generation understand that their approaches to life (which worked so well in the past) are not as effective as they once were, they are unsure how to adapt to the life that confronts them in the 21st century.

We need a new mindset that enables us to function in a world where constantly increasing change is the norm. We need a new mental approach to life that empowers us to anticipate change and prepare for it. This world of exponential growth is exerting great pressure on our 20th-century paradigm for life—a paradigm forged in another time when the growth in change was linear. The only way to cope with modern life is to look at the world from a completely new perspective. The question is, of course, how do you do it?

The answer is that you do it by learning to live life like a quarterback. Consider what is going through the mind of a quarterback when he drops back to pass the ball. The quarterback sees the world around him on a split screen. On one side of this screen are all the things that are happening right now. These are the developments that affect his life in the short term, and for a quarterback they are urgent. He must deal with the linebacker who is blitzing around the end of the offensive line and the fact that one of his receivers has fallen down. If he doesn't respond to this immediate reality, in a split second he will be lying flat on his back wondering what day it is. He must adjust his thinking and step into the pocket created by the linemen blocking for him and look for other receivers, or he won't have enough time to make the play.

On the other side of this split screen is a remarkably different display. On this side of the screen, the quarterback sees the future. He's anticipating, visualizing, and imagining where things are going to be several seconds into the future, because to make a completed pass he must deal with a moving target. His receivers are running at full speed, making sudden changes to the direction they are going. That's why he can't throw the ball to where the receiver is at this very moment; if he does, the ball will arrive after the receiver has moved to a new position. To complete the pass, the quarterback has to throw it to where the receiver is going to be several seconds from now. He must envision where the receiver will be and then work backward in his mind to determine what he is going to do in the present to make that future event a reality.

A quarterback deals with the immediate reality just to survive, and because he is working with moving targets, he also deals with the future to ensure success. This is a very important point for everyone struggling with the exponential change in modern life. Our difficulties parallel those of the quarterback. We must deal with the world of the present just to survive. We must pay the mortgage, do the grocery shopping, and get the car fixed. We must gather supplies for tomorrow's English lesson, compile report card grades, and return a phone call to that unhappy parent. Neglecting any of these immediate tasks has very real and direct consequences. We must deal with all the urgent issues and tasks that come up on a daily basis just to survive.

To determine the long-term direction of our lives and the long-term goals we set for our instruction, we must split the screen in our mind and look to the future. Why? Because just like the quarterback, we are now dealing with a moving target. The world is changing exponentially, moving faster and faster every day. There is no way we can survive in this world if we only deal with the present. If we just focus on what exists right now, then by the time we have reacted to the current state of things, the world will have moved significantly to a new position. In a world on the move, there is no way you can be successful by dealing only with the present. You must split the screen in your mind and devote half of your attention to the future.

That side of the screen must anticipate, visualize, and imagine where the world will be in the future. From that vision of the future, we must then work backward to determine what we need to do right now to help prepare our students for that future, which will arrive very quickly. In their book, *Understanding by Design*, Grant Wiggins and Jay McTighe (2005) say that success in modern life must focus on future needs and that mapping our way back from the future to where we are now is the only way to get a real handle on what we need to do today to prepare for tomorrow. This is crucial for educators because our mandate is to create instructional experiences that will prepare students for success in the world they will graduate into. For that reason, education is very much an endeavor focused on the future.

> *The world is changing exponentially, moving faster and faster every day. There is no way we can survive in this world if we only deal with the present.*

In her book of the same name, Jennifer James calls this "thinking in future tense" (1996). It requires a significant shift in the way we view the world on one side of our split screen. Effective educators use their intuition to make a reasoned extrapolation of what students will need to operate in the world of tomorrow based on current trends. In this way, the future informs our present to guide our instruction.

This is much more easily said than done, because our lives are often driven by the tyranny of the urgent things that arise every day. It takes considerable effort to prepare students for the next class, the next day, the next topic, the next test, the next term, and to meet the mandates of educational legislation, let alone to deal with the responsibilities of our personal lives. At times these urgent demands can overwhelm us. In such circumstances, it is a major victory just to get through the day. Dealing with the present is not enough. It is also our job to prepare the next generation for success in their future lives. It is critical that we develop this split-screen view of the world if we hope to adequately prepare our students for what awaits them.

The world is no longer the static, predictable place it was during the late Industrial Age. It is now a moving target that is picking up speed. We must start looking at where the world is going to be, not just where it is. To do this, we must all learn to use our intuition. By this, we are not referring to some sort of mystical crystal ball gazing. On the contrary, what we are referring to here is a highly rational process of making reasoned extrapolations based on major trends that are now unfolding. We must consider life through the lens of emerging technologies. When we begin to live our lives this way, we are able to constantly look into the future.

Looking for Trends

So let's do it. Let's try to get an idea of where the world is heading over the next 10 to 15 years. By putting what we know about change and technology together, we can begin to see what is coming. There are six major trends in technological development that we simply can't ignore. They are: (1) Moore's Law, (2) photonics, (3) the Internet, (4) InfoWhelm, (5) nanotechnology, and (6) biotechnology. We will explore several of these trends in the following chapters.

Summarizing the Main Points

- The only way to cope with modern life is to look at the world from a completely new perspective.

- In a world on the move, there is no way you can be successful by dealing only with the present. You must split the screen in your mind and devote half of your attention to the future.

- Effective educators use their intuition to make a reasoned extrapolation of what students will need to operate in the world of tomorrow based on current trends.

- We must start looking at where the world is going to be, not just where it is.

- There are six major trends in technological development that simply can't be ignored: (1) Moore's Law, (2) photonics, (3) the Internet, (4) InfoWhelm, (5) nanotechnology, and (6) biotechnology.

Some Questions to Consider

- What kind of mental approach will help you survive and thrive in exponentially changing times?

- What different skills will kids need to operate successfully in this new world?

- What does it mean to be thinking "in future tense"?

- What areas do students need to address to live effectively and successfully now and in the future?

- What major challenges will students face in tomorrow's constantly changing world that they don't face now?

- Based on what you have just read, what are three things you have learned today, and how will you use them?

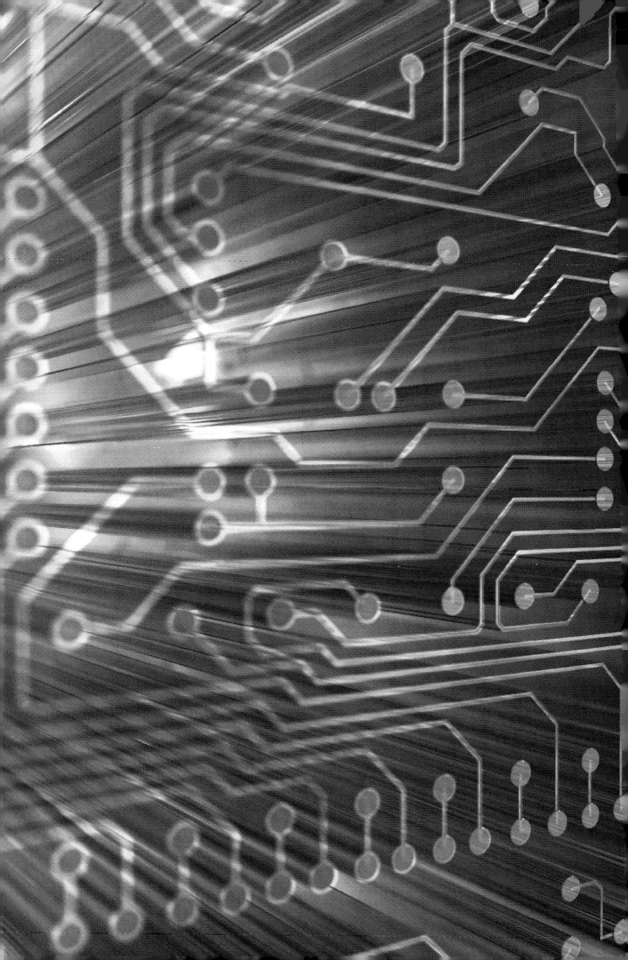

Chapter 5
Trend 1: Moore's Law

> The technology at the leading edge changes so rapidly that you have
> to keep current after you get out of school.
>
> **Gordon Moore**

Gordon Moore, one of the inventors of the integrated circuit, was the co-founder, chief
research scientist, and then chairman of Intel Corporation, the leading manufacturer of
microchips for computers in the world today. In 1965, four years before he co-founded Intel,
he wrote an article in *Electronics* magazine in which he proposed the theory of Moore's Law.
He believed that based on the technology available at the time, the processing power and
speed of any electronic computational device would double every 24 months, while at the
same time the price to produce that device would decline by 50 percent. In other words,
every 24 months we had technology that was twice as powerful at half the price. This is
exponential (as opposed to linear) growth.

Let's consider how this prediction has played out. In 1978, using a computer meant operating
a minicomputer that had 8K of RAM. Keep in mind that it takes 1024K to make one megabyte
(1MB). Back in 1978, you could buy a computer with 8K of RAM for $250,000 to $350,000. The
following year, personal computers burst onto the scene, and sales went through the roof. All
of a sudden PCs appeared on the market. Let's look at the average computer in 1979.

Moore's Law
(Doubling every 24 months)

Year	1979
RAM	8K
Storage	128K
Speed	2MHz
Cost	$5,000

If you were one of the few people using a computer at that time, the big decision was
whether you would have 8K of RAM or go out and sell the house and put in 16K of RAM. Back
then, 16K was a lot of RAM, but it was nice to know you had more than you would ever need.
Back then, you didn't have a hard drive, you had a 5¼-inch floppy disk that held 128K. This
is the equivalent of 40 pages of single-spaced text. No font variety, no graphics, no colors, no
images. Just plain old text. The speed was an astonishing 2 megahertz (MHz), which meant

that it was *really, really slow*. So slow, in fact, that you could start your computer and then refinance the mortgage, re-roof and re-side your house, and by then, if there wasn't an input–output error, you might be up and running. Interestingly, the same machine that one year earlier would have cost $250,000 to $350,000 was reduced to $5,000, so it was quite a bargain. Now, let's fast-forward five years to 1984.

Moore's Law
(Doubling every 24 months)

Year	1979	1984
RAM	8K	128K
Storage	128K	400K
Speed	2MHz	10MHz
Cost	$5,000	$3,900
1024K = 1MB		1024MB = 1GB

By 1984, the average computer had increased dramatically from 16K of RAM to 128K of RAM. The disk drive capacity had swelled from 128K to 400K. The speed had exploded from 2MHz to a blistering 10MHz. Yet, despite the fact that at the time inflation was more than 16 percent and interest rates were close to 20 percent, the price had dropped from $5,000 to less than $3,900. In 1986, Gordon Moore wrote one of a series of articles in which he had to repeatedly revise Moore's Law based on the remarkable developments in chip technology that had occurred in the previous few years. As a result, Moore suggested that the technology could squeeze twice as many transistors onto an integrated circuit every 18 months while at the same time the cost of creating the chips decreased by half—thus increasing the speed and capacity of the chips by a factor of 4 every 18 months. As a result, a lot has happened between 1986 and today. There is almost no way to keep a current chart accurate, though it will help to demonstrate exponentialism very well. Because this chart was prepared in June 2010, it probably looks much older than that to you because the machine described is old technology to you now.

Moore's Law
(Doubling every 18 months)

Year	1979	1984	2010
RAM	8K	128K	2GB
Storage	128K	400K	350GB
Speed	2MHz	10MHz	2.5GHz
Cost	$5,000	$3,900	$400
1024K = 1MB		1024MB = 1GB	

Try finding a new computer today with less than 2GB of RAM. If you buy a 2GB computer, you probably won't regret it for at least a month. If you don't have a 250GB hard drive, where are you going to store all of those pictures, movies, and music that you're downloading? If your computer isn't running 2GHz or more, you're going to wait forever for your software to load. As Moore's Law predicted, the prices continue to decline at the same time that power and performance continue to accelerate. Stop for a moment and consider the previous table. When you consider the figures, do you see any kind of trend emerging? Our point will be again and again that you can't view any trend or any technology outside of the continuum from where it's been to where it is to where it will be.

Is There More Moore?

Most of us feel overwhelmed by technology today—we feel that we are way behind, so our focus tends to be on now, which really means on the past. The critical question to ask is, given these trends, what does the future hold? Who better to ask than Gordon Moore, who is now retired. Recently, he was interviewed by *Wired* magazine and was asked the same question he's been asked for more than 40 years: "What is the future of Moore's Law?"

So far, Moore's prediction has been uncannily accurate, but it's very hard to grasp the significance of Moore's Law because we tend to think linearly and not exponentially. What he continues to say is staggering. He suggests that just based on the scientific principles that hold up Moore's Law, the exponential doubling of Moore's Law is going to continue for at least another 15–20 years. Additionally, recent announcements in the field of molecular electronics lead many experts in the field to believe that the exponential doubling of Moore's Law is going to continue for at least another 50 and probably another 100 years.

If you extrapolate out, the future is going to be unbelievable. When we look at the numbers, we are not concerned about how prepared we are for this future, but how prepared our children will be. What does the future hold for the children who enter kindergarten in 2010—the kids who will be part of the graduating class of the year 2022? Just based on a reasoned extrapolation of Moore's Law (and ignoring all other global exponential change forces), what kind of technology will be common to them? What kind of technology will be common to us all, one generation out?

Moore's Law
(Doubling every 18 months)

Year	1979	1984	2010	2022
RAM	8K	128K	2GB	208TB
Storage	128K	400K	350GB	40TB
Speed	2MHz	10MHz	2.5GHz	1.2THz
Cost	$5,000	$3,900	$400	$1.37

1024K = 1MB   1024MB = 1GB   1024GB = 1TB

Imagine a computer with 200,000MB of RAM, a 40-terabyte hard drive, blazing along at 600,000MHz plus. If this computer were available today, would you be willing to purchase it for $1.37?

As Marc Prensky (2006) notes, because of Moore's Law, students one generation out will work with technology that will be in excess of 1 billion times more powerful than the technology we commonly use today. Based on current trends, and given that we live in exponential times, the bigger question has to be what's next?

As nanotechnology and new and emerging three-dimensional chip technology design techniques become available in the next few years, it is absolutely certain that Moore's Law will continue to accelerate. In fact, Moore's Law has again been revised recently. He now says doubling is occurring every 12 months and accelerating. Given what has already happened, what do you think these technologies will look like one generation of students out?

Moore's Law
(Doubling every 12 months)

Year	2010	2018
RAM	2GB	2,097,152GB
Storage	350GB	209,715,200GB
Speed	2.5GHz	524,288,000GHz
Cost	$400	3¢

1024K = 1MB	1024MB = 1GB	1024GB = 1TB

Based on current trends, at a minimum, one generation of students out, we will likely be looking at technologies that will be measured in terms of billions, if not trillions, of times more powerful than the technology we commonly use today.

▸ Prensky refers to most people of our generation as "Digital Immigrants," since we can remember when these technologies did not exist. Many of us can easily remember a time before the Internet, cell phones, fax machines, and maybe even computers. Throughout our lives, change has been relatively gradual. It's only in the last 10 years or so that we have really started to feel the momentum of exponential growth.

Because of exponentialism, things have not only changed, but they continue to change, and to do so exponentially. As a result, we will continue to experience change at an unprecedented rate. We can't continue to deny that it is happening and that it will continue to happen. For students today, both young and old, the Digital Generation have been born into the new digital landscape. For them, there has never been a time when these powerful technologies and resources have not existed. As a result, they have become Digital Natives, who have internalized the new digital landscape and have come to take it for granted.

If you have attended our presentations you have likely seen some strange things—innovative new computers, virtual projectable keyboards, MP3 players the size of a quarter. That's just the start! There are cell phones that are as small as a business card and some with built-in projection units; motion pens using gyroscopes to track your handwriting and transform it into typewritten text; projectors the size of a penny; mobile phones with expandable screens; Dick Tracy watches; bendable electronics paper; opto-electronic contact lenses that will form images such as words, charts, photographs, and videos in front of the eye; prototype vehicles that drive and brake exclusively controlled by a joystick; invisibility cloaks; antigravity machines; and the list goes on and on.

When you see devices like these, keep in mind that we live in exponential times and you will begin to understand that you are probably looking at history. By the time these items are available for public consumption, in all likelihood there are already three or four (possibly even five) generations of prototypes of these devices being developed in production labs around the world. The technology we, as consumers, will use for the next 10 years has essentially been invented—you just can't buy it yet.

Don't Get Comfortable With That Device, It's Being Replaced

Despite the fact that we now see that some of these devices have some power, we are simply not prepared for what's about to unfold. We are now going faster than human beings can endure. The pace of business and society can no longer keep up with the physics of chip technology. There was a time when punch cards were the only way to get information into a computer. When Apple launched the Macintosh computer, we moved to the era of the mouse and keyboard. The mouse has had 25 years in the spotlight, but that's changing. In 2007, Apple released a revolutionary product, the iPhone. Its multi-touch display, so simple and intuitive, seemed the natural way to interact with a computer, just by touching it. In a matter of mere months, dozens of other devices copied this interface of multi-touch and gestures. In 2010, the launch of the iPad signaled the beginning of the end for the mouse, and QWERTY may be going the way of the typewriter. Time is compressing and the life span of new technologies is becoming shorter.

By 2022, the power of an off-the-shelf computer will exceed the intelligence of a human being. By 2030, children will carry devices in their backpacks or their pockets containing the sum total of all human intelligence with any single piece of information accessible in a fraction of a second.

The End of Our Current Paradigm

If you want to read something that will absolutely blow your mind, read Ray Kurzweil's book and see the movie, *The Singularlity Is Near*. Kurzweil, besides being an incredible inventor and prolific writer, has been absolutely on the money for more than 30 years in projecting where new technologies and trends are going.

Kurzweil says the time is near when exponential technological change will be so rapid and so profound that it will fundamentally and irrevocably transform our world in unimaginable ways. Some experts would say that we can't comprehend this scale of change, at least with our current levels of understanding and that it is, therefore, virtually impossible to look past today and try making sense of what lies ahead.

What Kurzweil says in *The Singularity Is Near* is that as Moore's Law inevitably starts to diminish as transistors get closer and closer together, we shouldn't worry because Moore's Law will have long been superseded by quantum wires, nanotechnology, nanotubes, silicon photonics, 3-D chip designs, DNA, and biologically based computing that will increase the speeds and capacities of future devices not by factors of hundreds or thousands, but by a factor of billions.

Nanotechnology—Better, Smaller, Faster

When a structure or material or device is developed with one of its dimensions smaller than 100 nanometers (a nanometer is equal to one-billionth of a meter), we are dealing with the matter on an atomic or molecular scale, which falls under the domain of nanotechnology.

The ENIAC *computer.* (Image source: http://www.cs.dartmouth.edu/farid/teaching/cs4/ summer.08/notes/historyofcomputing/)

The photograph above is the Electronic Numerical Integrator And Computer (ENIAC)—the world's first digital computer, which was turned on for the very first time on Valentine's Day, 1946, at the University of Pennsylvania in Philadelphia. The ENIAC was a building-based computer; it was literally the size of a building. It was two floors high—one floor was just for the cooling system and the other floor was for the computer. ENIAC weighed 30 tons and was 8 feet high and 100 feet long (the length of two tractor trailer rigs put end to end). It cost $750,000 in 1946 and took a team of 10 people to operate it. At the time, it was a marvel, capable of performing fourteen 10-digit calculations per second.

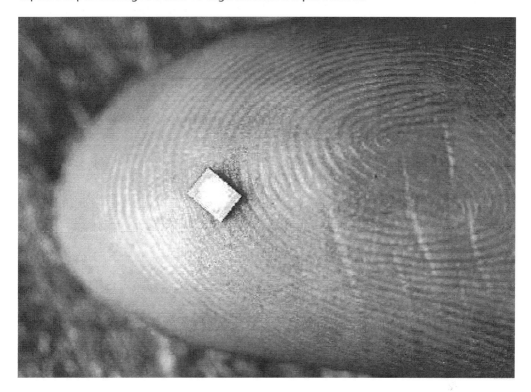

Image source: http://threeminds.organic.com/2008/12/

The photograph above shows a prototype chip from Intel—this is microtechnology. This chip is ⅛ inch by ¹⁄₁₆ inch in size. It could be made smaller, to the point where the chip could be accidentally inhaled without a person even realizing that it had been done. The point is, this chip is 10 million times more powerful than the building-based ENIAC from 1946. Imagine if we were to take a smartphone or laptop computer back in time to ENIAC's lab in February 1946. They'd think we were from another dimension!

Compare this to the fact that in 1966, it was noted that electronic calculators would never be able to compete with the computational ability of the human brain. In 1997, it was stated that there was no good evidence that most uses of computers significantly improved teaching and learning and that most schools would be better off if they just threw their computers into dumpsters.

By 2007, there were billions of transistors on a single microchip. Today, more and more devices are placed onto increasingly tinier pieces of electronic real estate and yet, today's devices will soon be obsolete. As chips become smaller, electronics will be embedded into our environment, woven into our clothing, and written directly to our retinas from eyeglasses and contact lenses.

There are currently hundreds of manufactured nanotechnology products on the market, and several more are added every week. A list of some these products is on the Project on Emerging Nanotechnologies web site (http://www.nanotechproject.org/). These include a wide range of things like stain- and wrinkle-resistant clothing, self-cleaning windows, glare-reducing and fog-resistant coatings for eyeglasses and camera lenses, sport socks and shirts that won't stink, cosmetics with particles designed to refract light and hide wrinkles, improved sunscreens, cutting boards and kitchen counters that kill bacteria, and cooking oil designed to be absorbed into food and transport vitamins and minerals.

Nanotechnology is currently being used to create nano-machines and nano-subs. These are microscopic computers, machines, and robots about the size of a virus, which can be swallowed or injected. If you have a clot or arterial clog, microscopic technology would make it possible to remove the blockages bloodlessly.

This will mean noninvasive surgeries of neurological systems. It will mean reprogrammed viruses and bacteria designed to deliver molecular doses of chemotherapy to target specific cells, allowing us to move from emergency interventions to deliberate and personal intervention.

In due course, this will lead to implantable diagnostic and treatment devices and biosensors. This leads the way for the creation of self-replicating machines that will reverse engineer human processes gone badly. We will have micromachines coursing through our bodies that will inspect, repair, and even rebuild dysfunctional parts of the nervous system.

We'll have brain pacemakers to silence neurons that malfunction in neurological disorders like epilepsy, and neural prostheses to replace more complicated body systems that have failed. Next, we'll move on to biomaterials laced with protein-based agents. Genes or stem cell therapies will be used to stimulate and perhaps outperform the body's natural ability to heal or reengineer memory tissues that were once thought impossible to repair.

It's Been a Long Time Coming

We know it's a lot to take in. You may be thinking that these are just wild guesses and a whole lot of science fiction. But Moore's Law is part of an exponential trend that has been happening for a very long time. It's only now, in our lifetime, that the technological doubling is visible to us.

Recall that commerce drove the Roman abacus to be used as early as 2400 BCE in Babylonia (http://en.wikipedia.org/wiki/history_of_computing_hardware), but modern mechanical calculating devices started with Blaise Pascal in 1642, with the first gear-driven calculator. Since then, there has been constant cycle of innovation as we have pursued faster and better calculation machines. The table on the following page shows how computational power has developed over time.

Computational Power Time Line

2400 BCE	Abacus
1600 CE	Gear-based calculators
1801	Punch card technology
1930	Electric mechanical calculators
1944	Mark 1 *10-digit multiplication in 3 seconds*
1942	ENIAC *10-digit multiplication in 3/1000 of a second (1,000 times faster)*
2007	IBM Blue Gene/L, 596 TFLOPS
2008	IBM, "Roadrunner," 1 petaflop
2009	Cray XT Jaguar, 1.75 petaflops
2012	Pleiades, 10 petaflops (in production)
2019	Cray, Inc., 1 exaflop (in production)

Source: http://en.wikipedia.org/wiki/FLOPS#Records

At the same time, the cost to produce these has dropped exponentially.

Cost of Production per Gflop

1961	$1,000,000,000,000
1984	$15,000,000
1997	$30,000
2000	$640
2003	$82
2007	42¢
2009	13¢

Going Vertical

The point here is that in exponential times, you cannot view any trend, any technology, any way of thinking outside of the exponential continuum from where it had come from to where it is heading. There is little doubt that we are going vertical. This has been happening for a long time, and there is no reason to believe it will suddenly stop.

This compels us as educators (which derives from the Latin *educere*—to lead out—literally, to lead children out of the educational wilderness) to look at things differently.

We have a tendency to think that change is something that happens somewhere else to someone else—that it happens to farmers, insurance agents, auto workers, office workers, and bankers—but that somehow we in education can continue to be immune to the effects of change. Our perception is that the future will be little more than a commonsensical linear extension of yesterday and today.

Remember that in exponential times, what is common sense today will not be common sense 20 years from now. Global exponential trends are not neutral, nor are they discriminating, and so they affect us all in different ways.

Moore's Law Is the Baseline

Even though Moore's Law—technological processing power and speed doubling exponentially ever 12 months—is absolute conceptual dynamite, it doesn't stop there. That's because the chip technology driving Moore's Law has led to a second global exponential trend, photonics. Over the last 20 years, depending on how you calculate it, photonics has actually grown four to six times the rate of Moore's Law. Now, that's fast!

Summarizing the Main Points

- The theory of Moore's Law as written in 1963: The processing power and speed of any electronic computational device would double every 24 months, while at the same time the price to produce that device would decline by 50 percent.

- In 1986, Moore suggested that the technology could squeeze twice as many transistors onto an integrated circuit every 18 months while at the same time the cost of creating the chips decreased by half.

- As Moore's Law predicted, the prices continue to decline at the same time that power and performance continue to accelerate.

- Recent announcements lead many experts to believe that the exponential doubling of Moore's Law is going to continue for at least another 50 to 100 years.

- Because of Moore's Law, students one generation out will work with technology that will be more than 1 billion times more powerful than the technology we commonly use today.

- The pace of business and society can no longer keep up with the physics of chip technology.

- Kurzweil says the time is near when exponential technological change will be so rapid and so profound that it fundamentally and irrevocably transforms our world in unimaginable ways.

- In exponential times, you cannot view any trend, any technology, any way of thinking outside of the exponential continuum from where it had come to where it is heading. We are going vertical.

- Photonics has grown at four to six times the rate of Moore's Law.

Some Questions to Consider

- What implications does Moore's Law hold for you personally and for your family?

- What implications does it hold for our communities?

- How will Moore's Law affect the nature of the workplace?

- Does this global exponential trend hold any implications for our schools and the children attending those schools?

- Given that this is a global trend, what skills will children need to have that we didn't need to have growing up?

- What will they need to be able to do with these skills?

- What are we doing in our schools right now to prepare children for a world that will be fundamentally different from the world we grew up in, or one that is fundamentally different than the one we live in now? Or do we think it doesn't really matter because our students are poor, or they speak English as a second language? Or worse, are we just pretending that these changes are not really happening, or that we've already dealt with it?

Chapter 6

Trend 2: Photonics

It would appear that we have reached the limits of what is possible to achieve with computer technology, although one should be careful with such statements, as they tend to sound pretty silly in 5 years.

John von Neumann, 1949

The first global exponential trend is Moore's Law, which asserts that technological processing power and speed doubles exponentially at least every 12 months. That kind of exponential growth is, by itself, absolute conceptual dynamite. Yet, it doesn't stop there. The computer chip technology that has driven Moore's Law for more than 40 years has led to the emergence of a second global exponential trend that, depending on how you calculate it, is growing at a rate faster than Moore's Law. This second trend is called *photonics*, which includes the generation, emission, transmission, modulation, signal processing, switching, amplification, detection, and sensing of light. Although photonics is a vast and complex science, let's narrow it down to telecommunications and information processing. In these applications we are primarily dealing with fiber-optic cable and the transmission of laser light of different colors and frequencies through that cable.

Consider this question for a moment: How fast is really fast bandwidth? Can you remember using a 300-baud, or a 1200-baud, or a 2400-baud, or 9600-baud modem? Do you remember moving from that to a 14.4, then a 28.8, and eventually a 56K modem? Each time, were you thinking you would never need any more speed?

In many communities, using the coaxial cable of a cable TV network, you can reach download speeds more than 15 megabits per second (mbps) when you're online by yourself late at night. Having a download speed of 15 mbps would be the equivalent of being able to completely fill the storage capability of a DVD in under 40 minutes. To help put that number into perspective, being able to completely fill the storage capabilities of a DVD would represent the work of a person typing at 100 words a minute, for 60 minutes an hour, 8 hours a day, 5 days a week, and 52 weeks a year, for almost 60 years. At our current speeds, we are downloading this content in less than 40 minutes.

The Need for Speed

Do you think this is fast? Well, it is not! Already, bandwidth speeds of 10 gigabytes per second (gbps) are becoming increasingly possible. A single strand of fiber-optic cable (glass fiber) is thinner than a single strand of hair, but it uses the scientific principles of photonics. It is possible to find download speeds in excess of 10 trillion bits or 10 gigabits per second. To be honest, we're actually underestimating what speeds are possible today.

Let's put this in perspective using our DVD example again: A download speed of 10 gbps is the equivalent of downloading the contents of 425 DVDs per second! Twenty years from now it is almost certain that bandwidth speeds will be measured in terms of billions, if not trillions, of times the speeds we have today.

How can we predict this? Because speed increases in photonics have closely followed that of Moore's Law. This makes sense if you think about it. Fiber-optic cable has almost unlimited potential. Data is transmitted at light speed, which is about as fast as it gets (at least in our current paradigm). The limiting factor of how much data gets transmitted are the chips on either end that transcode and transmit the information. Increasing bandwidth speeds is as simple as popping off the microchips at both ends and swapping them out for newer, faster ones, which are continuously being created in accordance with Moore's Law.

Look Mom, No Wires!

This is just talking about fiber optics; we aren't even taking into account the growing power of wireless fidelity (WiFi) for stores, homes, offices, and schools. Today, the standard is WiFi, but faster wireless protocols like WiMax, Ultra Wideband, LTE, and WiBro are coming onto the market.

In dozens of communities in the United States and Canada, cell phone companies are rolling out their 4G networks, with real-world peak speeds as fast as 50 mbps. Do you see what's happening? Just a short time ago, high-speed wired connections of 15 mbps seemed fast, but we have tripled that speed with the wireless technology available today. As the 4G networks become active and available in more places, the speed of wireless will be faster than fiber optic and unlimited in its reach.

Keep in mind that we are living in exponential times, just like Moore's Law indicates. Bandwidth can't be viewed just for what it is today, but has to be seen as part of the exponential continuum from the past to the future. So, the fundamental question that needs to be asked is, where is this all leading?

The answer is that the Internet will be everywhere. Regardless of where we are, be it driving in a car at 70 mph or flying in a plane at 40,000 feet, we will be perpetually connected online. This will quickly lead to an explosion of new, portable wireless technologies and services that will be beyond our imaginations.

Fiber-optic, wireless, and coaxial cable have become the concrete and steel of the information highway and will greatly affect the future of our global economy. It is safe to suggest that the technological and informational transformations of our recorded history to date will be dwarfed by the transformations we will witness in the next three to five years of our lives.

Although things are changing rapidly, this is just the beginning. These global exponential changes will have a profound effect upon every aspect of our lives, including the way we work, the way we live, the way we communicate, and especially the way we learn.

The Global Commuter

In her book, *The Death of Distance*, writer Frances Cairncross (1997) wrote that as a result of exponentially increasing bandwidth, the barriers to instantaneous communications are being brought down. As a result, we are experiencing the death of distance. Global exponential change is why everyone and everything has now become connected to everyone and everything else. Twenty years ago, high school and college graduates only had to compete for jobs with graduates from the neighboring communities. Ten years ago, these same graduates had to compete with graduates from neighboring states and provinces. Today, in the global economy, the competition comes directly from people (and increasingly from machines) in places like Shanghai, China; Mumbai, India; Tel Aviv, Israel; and Singapore. Soon, competition will come from anyone, anywhere on the planet.

In his book, *The World Is Flat*, Thomas Friedman (2005) asserts that the world is just that: it is increasingly flat. Because it is flat, today's economy is no longer bound by state, national, or geographical borders. It is not limited to or driven by manufactured goods or natural resources, and it does not rely solely on services. This new global economy has a strange new vocabulary with words like outsourcing, insourcing, crowdsourcing, offshoring, and supply chaining.

Up until now, our understanding of outsourcing was having manufactured goods produced in another country where labor is cheaper. This has led us to the delusion that a good education and a white-collar job will give us security. In his book, *Linchpin*, Seth Godin (2010) refers to this as "the myth of the white-collar job."

With a global communication structure that allows for information to be shared instantaneously, software designers in Wheeling, WV, are just as likely to be competing for work with software designers in Bangladesh as with designers in Silicon Valley. The competition is heavy for jobs of all kinds, not just high-tech jobs; fields such as tax preparation, CT scan analysis, and legal work, to name only a few, are experiencing this phenomenon.

Spend a few minutes on oDesk (www.odesk.com) and you can hire one of millions of professionals in every conceivable industry. We are already in a dramatically different workplace, and this new economy is based on new, not just reconstituted, skills and knowledge. This new knowledge requires a completely different vision for education in the 21st century. If our students are going to survive, let alone thrive, in a world that is increasingly flat, they will have to leave school with a completely different set of skills, knowledge, and habits of mind than the skill set they typically leave schools with today.

Tom Sawyer in the Digital Age

When Tom Sawyer persuaded his friends to give him a large marble in exchange for the privilege of whitewashing the fence for him, he was crowdsourcing. A relatively new phenomenon that evolved from our constant digital connection, crowdsourcing is a form of outsourcing where tasks traditionally performed by an employee are done by a large number of people, often for free.

Facebook and many other companies have been using crowdsourcing to have their users help in the translation of their products. This means a rapid development cycle and also keeps the language more compatible with current culture.

In 2008, the state of Texas announced a plan to install 200 cameras along the Mexico border. The idea is that anyone with an Internet connection and the willingness to participate could monitor the border for alleged illegal immigrants and report the activity.

The Canadian mining group Goldcorp posted 400MB of data online and offered a $575,000 prize to anyone who could analyze it and tell them where to dig. Goldcorp states the project produced 110 targets that yielded 8 million ounces of gold worth about $3 billion.

The best known example of crowdsourcing would be Wikipedia, a massive online project to provide general reference, news, and articles. The accuracy of Wikipedia has been proven to be greater than that of the *Encyclopedia Britannica*. Thousands of contributors edit and maintain this resource in real time. As news happens, as new scientific breakthroughs alter facts, Wikipedia is kept current by its army of volunteer contributors.

Through crowdsourcing, we can access the expertise and labor of the entire planet, or at least anyone with an Internet connection and some spare time to contribute. Now, not only do we compete against other experts in other parts of the world through outsourcing, but through crowdsourcing we compete against a labor market that is free. Remember, the profound changes that we are describing here are based on today's bandwidth. If we understand that the development of bandwidth is not static, but rather exists on the exponential continuum from the past to the future, what does the future hold?

More Technology Trends

The authors use software for the iPhone and computers called Continuous Voice Recognition (CVR). With CVR technology, you spend a few hours training it, and then while you speak 70 to 80 words per minute, the software will distinguish with 95 percent accuracy between you saying, "Recognize speech" and "Wreck a nice beach" and convert your words into text.

What does that have to do with the writing process? We are moving from the writing process to the speaking process. Now we're seeing the emergence of automated speech translation technology, or automated interpreting telephony. For example, imagine speaking into your phone and three seconds later having your words coming out at the other end in the language of the other person. If you don't believe me, go out to the Apple Store and buy Jibbigo. It's like having a live interpreter in your pocket. The software can handle translating both languages simultaneously to facilitate conversations—and it isn't limited to certain phrases and expressions—it's armed with a dictionary of 40,000 words and performs well if you limit yourself to one or two sentences at a time. Unbelievable! And that's just what we have at our disposal right now!

What does this do for people who speak English as a second language? How will we communicate in the future? How does this change the notion of being a tourist? What does this do to the idea of engaging international commerce?

You See a Problem, I See an Opportunity

We could go on and on, but the point is this: We want our students to excel, to thrive, and to survive. We must understand that social and intellectual capital are the new economic values in the world economy. The ability to memorize and regurgitate information, to perform low-level cognitive tasks, will not be enough—it's already not enough.

It would be easy to throw our arms up and say it's hopeless. If you alter your perspective slightly, things will look quite a bit different. In our paradigm, being employed meant getting an education, finding an employer, submitting a resume, being interviewed, getting the job, and then keeping our heads down and doing what we were told until we retire. It's safe, but extremely boring. Or at least it was safe—not so anymore. As we've gone through in detail, numerous jobs in various industries are moving or being replaced by other sources. This does not mean the end; instead it means a fabulous new beginning.

The new paradigm of today means that anyone can be remarkable. Anyone with an idea can contribute, can build the next greatest thing, can unite and lead a group of people, can connect collaborative partners around the world, and can access the best and brightest minds of our time in a way that is faster, easier, and more exciting then ever before. More importantly, anyone can develop and deliver the product they envision.

This is not a time to be afraid, but rather to embrace change. It's going to be a wild and crazy ride. However, our students need the skills to be able to capitalize on these opportunities— skills they are not being taught today. The great challenge for education is to prepare students for a world that doesn't yet exist, to equip them for solving problems that we haven't even begun to think about, and to train them to use technologies that haven't yet been invented.

Summarizing the Main Points

- The chip technology driving Moore's Law has led to a second global exponential trend called photonics.

- Both wired and wireless bandwidth speed capabilities are growing at an exponential rate.

- Increased bandwidth capabilities has led to the death of distance and the flattening of our world.

- Along with growing bandwidth capability, powerful new technologies have appeared that allow users to do things that would have been unimaginable even a few years ago.

- Because of the death of distance and the flattening of our world, students need to leave school with a completely different skill set than the skills needed by us and our parents.

Some Questions to Consider

- In a global economy, how does the idea of anytime, anywhere high-speed access to information and services change the skills, knowledge, and habits of mind that students would need to process massive amounts of readily available, but occasionally inaccurate, information?

- In a global economy where these students will be competing with people and machines from other countries, what skills, knowledge, and habits of mind will they need that older generations didn't need growing up?

- What should educators be doing to prepare students for the world that awaits them?

- What steps can we take to ensure that all of our students develop essential skills, including creativity training, to succeed in this emerging exponential environment?

- Consider that your thinking is probably based on linear common sense. Now, reconsider these questions based on exponential thinking.

Chapter 7
Trend 3: The Internet

> The Internet is the single most important development in the history of human communications since the invention of "call waiting."
>
> **Dave Barry, in *Dave Barry in Cyberspace* (1996, p. 121)**

So far we've examined two global exponential trends. The first is Moore's Law, which states that technological processing power and speed are doubling every 12 months while the cost to produce the technology is cut in half. The chip technology created by Moore's Law over the last 30 years has led to photonics, the second global exponential trend. Because of photonics, data transfer rates are growing at a rate even faster than Moore's Law. Moore's Law and photonics have created a ripple effect culminating in the third global exponential trend: the Internet Revolution.

Start of the Internet Boom

We take the Internet for granted. We think nothing of accessing our bank accounts, downloading music and books, tracking an impending thunderstorm, or checking email from just about anywhere in the world. But consider this: In 1990, there were fewer than 300 users of the World Wide Web on the planet. In 1995, the World Wide Web entered into public consciousness because of the launch of the web browser called Netscape Navigator. Do you recall when you first logged on?

At the end of 1994, Mosaic was launched as the first web browser. However, Mosaic Communications Company was forced by the University of Illinois to change its name. Mosaic became Netscape Navigator and launched in 1995. Seemingly overnight, the Internet appeared as a commercial force. Visiting "chatrooms" or "surfing the Net" were very popular activities. A few short years later, we have internalized the Internet. It has permeated every aspect of our lives, and we can't imagine how we survived without it. In fact, today there is a big push by the United Nations (http://en.wikipedia.org/wiki/Internet_access), who want Internet access to be considered a human right!

The Internet Today

According to Internet usage statistics (note that this estimate will be outdated by the time you finish reading this page) found at http://Internet-statistics-guide.netfirms.com/, there are more than two billion regular users in more than 180 countries. That is more than one in four around the world—25 percent of the world's population. As of this writing, the Web contains more than 100 billion web pages, and approximately 164,000 new users (that's about 113 per minute) are added in a typical 24-hour period. According to *Internet World Statistics*, the average web page is accessed 300 billion times a day.

As a result, conservatively, it is estimated that the Web is doubling in size every 120 days, which means that it's exponentially doubling in size three times per year! Take a moment to think about what this means—more than 80 percent of the sites that will exist a year from now don't exist today. This is massive growth, and as a result, the amount of bandwidth being used to accommodate this is estimated conservatively to be tripling exponentially every year. So what are some of the indicators of the exponentially growing power of the Internet? Let's take a look at some of the Internet's largest and fastest growing phenomena, including social networking sites, YouTube, Wikipedia, Skype, eBay, and virtual learning environments (VLEs). Note: Whatever statistics we provide will inevitably be outdated by the time this book is published, but this should give you some idea of trends.

Social Networking

Facebook

Six years ago, the social networking site Facebook didn't exist. Today, there are more than 500 million users on Facebook. Users share more than five billion pieces of content (web links, news stories, blogs, photos) on Facebook every week. They upload three billion photos a month and post 60 million status updates every day. The typical user spends 55 minutes on Facebook daily (and many, many hours engaged in Mafia Wars or Farmville). Facebook now accounts for one in four online pageviews (http://drakedirect.blogspot.com/2009/10/draft-facebook-article.html). Sites like Facebook are growing at almost three million new users per week worldwide. So you might be wondering, what kind of impact has this had on our society? It's significant. It's estimated that more than one out of every seven (14 percent) couples married in the United States in 2009 met for the first time online. Facebook launched Togetherville.com in 2010 as a supervised social networking site for children under the age of 10. It allows them to engage family and friends, share artwork, or play games. According to *Wired* magazine, Togetherville.com ". . . brings parents into the same virtual space as their children to help them mentor kids to be good digital citizens" (*Wired*, May 19, 2010).

Twitter

Twitter is a social networking and microblogging service that enables its users to send and read messages known as tweets. Tweets are text-based posts of up to 140 characters displayed on the author's profile page and delivered to the author's subscribers, who are known as followers. Senders can restrict delivery to those in their circle of friends or, by default, allow open access. It may seem that 140 characters is very limiting—think of it as an Internet haiku.

Since its creation in 2006, Twitter has gained notability and popularity worldwide as a tool for such things as finding assistance, political campaigning, legal proceedings, protesting and politics, public relations, and disseminating information. Many people struggled with Twitter for a long time trying to understand what it really was about. During a two-week period in June 2009, its purpose became clear. First there were the election demonstrations in Iran with people delivering information in real time. Two weeks later Michael Jackson died, something we may have previously heard about on television or from a coworker. However, on that day, the news that Michael Jackson had died flew around the Internet. Before the story could reach the news, the whole world knew.

Voice and Video

YouTube

Users of the Internet who want to connect with each other are not limited to the typed word. Anyone can post a video to the web site YouTube. As of this writing, YouTube is estimated to hold in storage at least 140,000,000 videos with 100,000,000 viewings of those videos every single day. To put those numbers into perspective, that's 70,000 videos being viewed every minute of every day. More than 20 hours of video are uploaded to YouTube every minute—that's about 10.6 million hours per year or about 1,300 years of content uploaded per year. We should pay careful attention to this trend. It indicates that video is rapidly replacing email, texting, and blogging.

iPods

Apple's iPod, and now iPhone, have changed the distribution of music, TV shows, and movies. Millions of songs, videos, audiobooks, movies, museum tours, academic courses, lectures, language lessons—almost anything imaginable—are available for download 24 hours a day, 7 days a week.

As of April 2010, the Apple Store had sold more than 10 billion songs, as well as more than 220 million iPods, 42 million iPhones, and 30 million iPod Touches. Apple's iTunes sells 5 million songs (that's 58 songs per second) and 50,000 movies a day. As a result, Apple, a company we think primarily sells computers, sells more music or media than any other company in the world. In just the past five years Apple has acquired 70 percent market share of digital music players and almost 90 percent of the digital music market. How do you think this has changed the music and movie industry?

Skype

Skype is a software application that allows users to make voice calls over the Internet. Calls to other users within the Skype service are free, and calls from Skype's service to traditional landline telephones and mobile phones can be made for a nominal fee using a debit-based user account system. Skype has also become popular for additional features, including instant messaging, file transfer, and video conferencing. Skype's number of registered users increased from 100,000 to more than 100,000,000 from 2008 to 2010. You can call anyone, anywhere, and have a videoconference with one or many people anywhere on the planet at any time for pennies or nothing at all. It is not uncommon to be on Skype at the same time as more than 20 million other users. In just a few years Skype has become the largest international voice carrier in the world and has profoundly affected the telecommunications industry (http://www.telegeography.com/cu/article.php?article_id=15656&email=html).

Online Shopping

It is estimated that seven out of 10 Americans has gone shopping online within the past 30 days and that one in three has bought something. Internet-related sales are close to a trillion dollars a year, which is twice the amount of sales by the American auto industry.

eBay

eBay, an online auction and shopping web site in which people and businesses buy and sell a broad variety of goods and services worldwide, had just 30 employees in 1998. Today it has 13,000 employees and more than 230 million customers worldwide engaged in 100 million auctions at any given time. It's a modern day worldwide yard sale—a flea market for buying and selling that never closes. Companies such as eBay and craigslist, a free classified ad service, have had a powerful influence on the way things are bought and sold. Around the world, a growing number of people make at least part of their income buying and selling using online auction services.

Wikipedia

Wikipedia is an online encyclopedia to which anyone can contribute. It contains more than 13 million articles in more than 250 languages. By comparison, the *Encyclopedia Britannica* has approximately 33,000 articles. More than one million new articles were posted on Wikipedia in 2009 alone. Its greatest strength is that, unlike *Encyclopedia Britannica*, when a news story breaks, it can be updated in real time. Wikipedia articles are added or edited more than 300,000 times per day, and more than 5,000 articles are deleted every day because they are unsubstantiated. There have been some legitimate concerns about the inaccuracy of some of Wikipedia's articles, so it still has a ways to go. On the horizon, however, a new academic version of Wikipedia is being developed. Beyond that, Wikiversity supports learning communities by offering a series of tutorials for the fostering of learning rather than formal content. The question is, does Wikipedia hold any potential for education?

Virtual Learning Environments (VLEs)

Second Life

Second Life is a virtual learning environment (VLE). Millions of participants have created avatars (virtual identities and personalities) that allow them to socialize, entertain, interact commercially, earn real money, and learn in self-contained virtual environments that are created almost entirely by Second Life's users. Avatars buy, sell, invest, and generate real wealth using a virtual monetary system called Linden Dollars.

Now you might think that this is just play, but this development is so significant that IBM, which already has 26,000 blogs and 20,000 internal wikis, has purchased more than 50 islands in Second Life. IBM refers to it as the 3-D Internet, and the company now offers orientations, classes, meetings, marketing, and training in Second Life. IBM thinks Second Life is the near and distant future of online business. They believe that companies and customers will transact business on the 3-D Internet. IBM hopes to make a great deal of money advising corporate clients on how to craft business strategies for virtual worlds. To this end, they have built several virtual retail centers in Second Life for major companies throughout the world.

Virtual Education

So does any of this really have implications for education? Yes! For example, at least 1,000 universities around the world teach courses or conduct research in Second Life. Several thousand courses are offered exclusively within it. In 2009, 40 graduates from

Buffalo's 150-year-old Bryant & Stratton College's online degree programs received their hard-earned degrees—online in avatar form on the college's Second Life virtual campus. There was a commencement speaker during the ceremony in avatar form, a procession, and the conferring of degrees to students whose avatars were even draped in digital caps and gowns. New educational institutions have also emerged that operate exclusively within Second Life, taking advantage of the platform to deliver a high-quality service to a worldwide audience at a very low cost.

Because there is always justifiable concern about younger, more vulnerable students, there is Teen Second Life. This application is set up in part for student projects like Global Kids Island, a place for teen residents to learn about important social and world issues. We must wonder how long it will be before these types of opportunities become available to compete directly with public schools.

Any student with an iPod and a wireless connection can watch and listen to a replay of the lesson again between classes or at almost any other time or place on the planet.

Course lectures, language lessons, lab demonstrations, sports highlights, and campus tours are also now available from iTunes University. More than 1,000 universities including Berkeley, Stanford, Duke, Cambridge, Oxford, Yale, and MIT use this technology. Classes are completely accessible and available as free downloads from Apple's iTunes store—often within five minutes of the lesson finishing. Any student with an iPod and a wireless connection can watch and listen to a replay of the lesson again between classes or at almost any other time or place on the planet.

Similar services are provided by sites such as YouTube EDU, Academic Earth, ResearchChannel, MIT World, TeacherTube, TED (Technology, Entertainment, Design), Udemy, and FORA.tv. All of these offer videos of lectures, online courses, and discussions that are provided by hundreds of universities, colleges, organizations, and corporations around the planet.

What we have described here is only a small sampling of the kinds of resources that are increasingly available online. What are the implications of the continued development of increasingly sophisticated resources for schools? How does digital multimedia content affect the notion of paper-based resources and paper-based learning? How does it change the purpose of libraries? Imagine the potential savings when textbooks and other materials are available in digital format that can be downloaded to a computer or handheld device and updated frequently rather than every five to seven years as they are in current models of the textbook adoption cycle. Well, eTextbooks already exist. For example, CourseSmart (www. CourseSmart.com) offers eTextbooks for nearly 7,000 U.S. colleges and universities. These can be viewed online or as downloadable PDFs. The eTextbooks are searchable and enabled for notes summary or other document without having to retype the content. Content can be shared with classmates online as well. The cost is half the price of the printed version.

Is it any wonder that many schools are quickly moving to 1:1 computing for their students? This certainly isn't a matter of being trendy; it's a matter of cost-effectiveness and pragmatics. Do kids today communicate differently online with email or instant messaging than older generations were taught to communicate in school? The answer is clearly yes. Given that these are increasingly the mediums of communication for kids, what have we done to change the language arts curriculum in schools today? Is the curriculum pretty much the same curriculum that we were taught, and even that our parents were taught?

What do kids read online—novels, essays, and poems? Or product summaries, news reports, commentary, analysis, gossip, statistics, tables, charts, graphs, and spreadsheets? Reading a novel, essay, or poem may have them literary reading from a screen. Reading product summaries, news reports, commentary, analysis, and statistics is what we call technical reading. Technical reading is actually a completely different cognitive process that uses a completely different part of the brain.

Given that information in the technical reading form is becoming more and more common, children today are as comfortable reading from a screen or a handheld device as we are reading from a book. Are we modifying the curriculum to prepare our students for this type of reading? Or are we pretending this isn't really happening because how children communicate, how they read, and how they choose to interact with information and one another don't conform to our traditional definition of literacy? If the world is experiencing such a massive, radical shift from traditional text-based learning resources to online interactive multimedia ones, how can we reorganize the curriculum to ensure that it aligns with the emerging world of digital and online learning?

What's Next?

There is a cyclical relationship between us and technology. New and advanced technologies are internalized so quickly that they become essential to us. There was a time that the microwave was a marvel; now we stand in front of it for an agonizing two minutes waiting for popcorn. As each new technology becomes part of us, it creates demand, and this demand pushes the envelope of the next wave of new technologies that will become essential. This cyclical symbiotic relationship starts all over again.

In the same way that new technologies have and will continue to dramatically change and grow in power, the Web is radically transforming. Ten years from now the Internet will be completely unrecognizable to us. Right now, most people use a mouse or a keyboard to access the Web. As wired and wireless bandwidth speeds increase, the Internet will become a working and learning environment where you'll put on a pair of virtual reality glasses or headgear (or more likely, it will be holographically projected for you). You will walk and talk your way through the Web, searching for information and interacting with digital devices.

We aren't there yet, of course. There is lots of criticism about slowness, security, under/over regulation, system overload, spam, and all the rest. These issues and emergent new issues will eventually be resolved. Just like the early telephone system, things aren't perfect, not all have the necessary access, and it's not always easy to use. Yet despite any remaining skeptics, the Internet continues to come at us like a freight train. In a few short years, it has reached full-fledged status as a commercial medium. Not to use the intelligent Web, not to acknowledge its power and potential, not to acknowledge that the Internet is and will continue to be a development of profound significance is a little like refusing to use a telephone because it's ruining our ability to write or refusing to use a car because we used to ride horses.

The kinds of things the Internet allows us to easily do and that we increasingly take for granted today would have been unimaginable even five years ago. The Internet is a business, education, entertainment, and communications center capable of fitting into a single device. In the past, we had to go different places and use different devices to do different things. We used the phone to talk to others; now we use Skype. We went to the post office to send and receive mail; now we use text messaging. We drove to a store to buy a newspaper or walked across the lawn to pick up the delivered paper, but now we check dozens of news sources on the Web for all the information, photos, statics, and editorials we could ever want. We went to the library to do research; now we use Wikipedia, Google Earth, Merriam-Webster Online, and hundreds of other sites for up-to-the-minute information. We went to school to learn; now we learn online. All these services are in one place and in one device. Instead of going to the services, we expect the services to come to us—anytime, anywhere.

The Internet Revolution has just begun. Yet it is starting to overwhelm us, outstripping our capacity to cope, antiquating our laws, transforming our morals, reshuffling our economy, reordering our priorities, redefining our workplace, testing our constitution, shifting our concept of reality, and making us sit for longer periods of time in front of glowing screens. At the same time, it is only marginally affecting teaching, learning, and assessment.

It does not stop here. The Information Age came together when powerful new technologies (Moore's Law) intersected with increasing wired and wireless bandwidth speeds (photonics) to create a global digital network (the Internet). These three factors together have led in the past few years to our fourth global exponential change force—InfoWhelm.

Summarizing the Main Points

- It is estimated that the Web is doubling in size every 120 days, which means that it's exponentially doubling in size three times per year, and the amount of bandwidth being used to accommodate this is estimated conservatively to be tripling exponentially every year.

- IBM believes that companies and customers will transact business on the 3-D Internet.

- Technical reading is a completely different cognitive process that uses a completely different part of the brain.

- As each new technology becomes part of us, it creates demand, and this demand pushes the envelope of the next wave of new technologies that will become essential.

- The Internet is a business, education, entertainment, and communications center capable of fitting into a single device.

- The Information Age came together when powerful new technologies (Moore's Law) intersected with increasing wired and wireless bandwidth speeds (photonics) to create a global digital network (the Internet). These three factors together have led in the past few years to our fourth global exponential change force—InfoWhelm.

Some Questions to Consider

- Consider how far the evolution of the Internet has come since its 1995 launch. What do you do online now that you didn't before the Internet entered your life? Has it made things easier or more difficult for you?

- Does what has been described have any implications for you? What implications does it hold for your family? For your community? For the way you play, work, and communicate?

- What are the most effective social tools that promote learning in schools? How do we use these tools effectively, and not just as a "cool thing"?

- Will the workplace and our homes increasingly be connected to wired and wireless high-speed connections to the Web?

- Will an increasing number of households have, and regularly use, computers?

- Will computers and related devices eventually become as common as telephones and television?

- Does this have any implications for the future of learning?

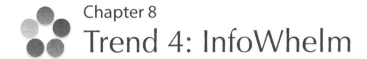

Chapter 8
Trend 4: InfoWhelm

> Getting information off the Internet is like taking a drink from a fire hydrant.
>
> **Mitchell Kapor**

The technological doubling created by Moore's Law has precipitated a parallel change in the knowledge base. Over the last decade this technological doubling has forced our societies to reorganize their knowledge. As a result, the boundaries between conventional disciplines are breaking down and altering the very fabric of our societies. This is fundamentally and forever changing the way we work, the way we play, the way we communicate, the way we view our fellow citizens, how we learn, and what's important for us to know.

InfoWhelm is the ever-widening gap between what we understand and what we think we should understand. A good rule of thumb is, the faster the world changes, the shorter the half-life of knowledge is and the greater the need to invest in lifelong learning. Knowledge today becomes obsolete incredibly fast. Therefore, in the age of InfoWhelm, what begins to matter more is not the ability to remember specific content, but rather the ability to place information in a context and use it effectively.

Because of exponential growth, we now live in the age of disposable information, where even the daily newspapers arrive out of date. Information has become a temporary and disposable commodity; it has value, but it is also just about as perishable as fruit. Information has a certain value today, but may have to be discarded if it is not used by tomorrow.

Let us try to put InfoWhelm quickly into perspective. In 2003, researchers at the University of California, Berkeley, tried to total the globe's information production by adding up all the ones and zeros that make up photos, videos, PDF files, email, web pages, instant messages, phone calls, and other digital stuff. Their estimate was that digital content throughout the infoscape had generated 5 exabytes of data—understanding that 5 exabytes of data would fill the Library of Congress, the world's largest library, to capacity with content 37,000 times. That in itself is amazing, but according to a paper released in 2009 by Boston's IDC, all the zeros and ones had generated not 5 exabytes, but 500 exabytes of digital information in just six years thanks to the growing percentage of users who have access to broadband, which has increased their ability to share and communicate information. That is a 10,000 percent increase in just a few years. Today, our data output has exceeded our ability to physically store it.

So what would 500 exabytes of data look like? If we printed it all into books, how many books would that be? What do you think? Would it be a stack of books as tall as the Empire State building or Mount Everest? Would it reach all the way to the moon or the sun? What if we told you it would reach all the way to Pluto—13 times? It's true! That's the equivalent of 237 billion fully loaded Amazon Kindle readers, 30 billion fully loaded Apple iPod Touches, 19 billion fully loaded Blu-ray DVDs, or enough paper to deforest the planet 12 times per year.

According to "As the Economy Contracts, the Digital Universe Expands," a white paper from IDC Digital Decade, at the current growth rate, that stack of books would be growing 20 times faster than the fastest rocket ever made, the Atlas V, which powered the NASA Pluto New Horizons spacecraft. It took that spacecraft 13 months to reach Pluto after it left Patrick Air Force Base on January 19, 2006. It would take this growing stack of books three weeks.

Today we can access far more information than we will ever need. According to a July 25, 2008 post on the official Google Blog (http://googleblog.blogspot.com/2008/07/we-knew-web-was-big.html), Google has by itself already processed links to more than 1 trillion unique URLs on the Web. Most of the information on every one of those pages is accessible in less than a second and is searchable in 100 languages. There are more than 3 billion Google searches performed every day (http://royal.pingdom.com/2010/01/22/internet-2009-in-numbers/), up from 150 million just 3 years ago. What did we do before Google?

How about a search for the topic of global warming? More than 31 million references to global warming in 0.11 of a second. Probably a few too many for many of us to read through.

How about a search for pictures of whales—5.6 million in 0.13 second? This too is probably overkill. If you're anything like us, you probably look at the first dozen or so links before your eyelids start to flutter.

How about a search for weather videos—600,000 in 0.17 second? Way more information than anyone needs or wants. This is InfoWhelm! No matter the topic, you can retrieve millions of references on it in mere seconds by searching Google. But Google doesn't just search for text, images, and video. Google has developed and provided, at no charge, hundreds of tools and services, including tools for text messaging, question answering, blogging, academic research, food recipes, phone numbers, addresses, images, satellite photos, financial information, maps, product information, and web services that will translate web sites from more than 100 languages into English.

Because of exponential growth, we now live in the age of disposable information, where even the daily newspapers arrive out of date.

There's also Google Books (http://books.google.com), which has digitized millions of books. Search for almost any book by almost any author and you will instantly get a summary of all the books or publications the author has been involved with. Perhaps the one that interests you is *Teaching the Digital Generation,* written by Ted McCain and Ian Jukes in 2008. Just click on the title and you will see the title page; click on the table of contents to view the chapters of the book. Suppose you want to search *Teaching the Digital Generation* for any references to the term *exponential.* Type the term into the book search tool and press return. A list of page numbers of every reference to the term *exponential* in the book will appear. If you're interested in a particular reference, just click on the page to read it at your leisure.

Consider the implications this kind of capability might have for research, for going to the library, for going to a bookstore. Bookstores will have to compete with the ease of being able to download an entire book over the Web at little or no cost. Checking out a library book could become as old-fashioned as using a pay phone, visiting a travel agent to book a flight, or sending a handwritten letter by post. If we interpret these developments in light of the exponential continuum, we can conclude that very soon we'll all have the same anytime, anywhere, digital access to information that iPods and iPhones have given us to music.

Think about Amazon's Kindle, which is essentially an iPod for information. The original Kindle is about the size of a slim paperback, but can store an entire library's worth of books, newspapers, magazines, blogs, PDF files, music, and images all downloaded wirelessly from the Internet. Its electronic screen provides an image as sharp and natural as ink on paper that produces neither glare nor eye strain. You can read it inside or outside. It weighs 2 pounds, can display 7,500 pages before needing a battery recharge, and uses an advanced cell phone technology. This means you don't need a WiFi hot spot. You can hear about a book and then download it in a matter of minutes from the Kindle Store, which at this writing has more than 500,000 books, newspapers, magazines, and blogs available in under 60 seconds (http://www.amazon.com/kindle-store-ebooks-newspapers-blogs/b?ie=UTF8&node=133141011). Ebooks typically cost one-quarter to two-thirds the price of paper versions. You could have your newspaper delivered wirelessly every morning or your monthly magazine delivered before it arrives at the newsstand. Instructors could upload their own lessons, articles, or units.

On a Kindle, it's also easy to search the entire personal library you hold in your hand. Simply type a word, the name of an author, or a phrase, and the Kindle will find every instance across your Kindle library of books, newspapers, magazines, or files. Do a search using Wikipedia, use the built-in dictionary, make annotations, highlight text, bookmark pages, or adjust text size. It will even read to you.

Depending on the source, somewhere between 1.3 and 3 million Kindles had already been sold by February 2010 (http://mobileopportunity.blogspot.com/2010/02/how-many-kindles-have-really-been-sold.html). But even as Kindle becomes familiar in the mainstream, because of Moore's Law and a device called the iPad, the Kindle may soon become ancient history.

Analysts estimate that as many as 16 million iPads will be sold in the next year, obliterating the Kindle and netbooks (http://www.electronista.com/articles/10/06/08/morgan.stanley.sees.ipad.already.slowing.netbooks/). The iPad is a paradigm shift in personal computing. Because of its simple developer's kit, anyone with a computer, some basic skills, and a few hours on his or her hands can write an application. Tens of thousands of applications were written for iPhone in the first year; it's likely the iPad will see even more. Newspapers, magazines, television, and more are streamlining their dying industries for web-based delivery. Only 10 days after launching their iPad application, the TV network ABC called it a huge success, stating that web-based delivery is more than a viable alternative. Shortly after that, in an attempt to stay relevant in the market, Amazon released a Kindle application for iPad. It may be too late, though; by June 7, two months after its release, the iBookstore had already grabbed more than 20 percent of eBook sales (http://www.electronista.com/articles/10/06/07/establishes.ipad. as.threat.to.kindle/).

Yet, even the iPad is not the end, but a new beginning. Undoubtedly more devices with more and different features will become available in the near future. Project a few years out. Imagine having a device in the palm of your hand or on your wrist. Can you imagine an implant in your nose that contains the sum total of human knowledge and gives the user access to any single bit of information—any piece of text, photograph, video, painting, TV or radio program, web page, blog post, or music produced by all the people of the world—in short, the entire works of humankind, from the beginning of recorded history, in all languages, accessible anywhere the user is on the planet within a fraction of a second? That is exactly where all these developments are leading. This is exactly what new technologies will allow us to do in the next few years.

> *Checking out a library book could become as old-fashioned as using a pay phone, visiting a travel agent to book a flight, or sending a handwritten letter by post.*

This begs some fundamental questions, though. What types of skills and knowledge will people need to have to effectively use such devices? What will individuals need to process massive amounts of digital information that will literally be at their fingertips?

Are our schools preparing students for this world? Right now the answer is no. Despite how our world has changed and continues to change, most of our schools and classrooms continue to operate the way they have for more than 100 years. Will we help students cope with InfoWhelm, or will we just continue to provide analog schools in a digital age?

Today, the digital generation is absolutely as comfortable, if not more comfortable, sending and receiving email and text messages, surfing the Web, and reading from a handheld device, cell phone, or computer screen as people of the older generations are reading from a book. How will anytime, anywhere access to new information affect students' lives? How will it change the way they work, the way they live, the way they communicate, and the way they learn? How do we modify the current curriculum to prepare students for this kind of anytime, anywhere access to multimedia information?

Why haven't we done it already? Perhaps it is because the way students today choose to communicate, prefer to read, and choose to interact with information and others doesn't conform to our traditional definitions of literacy.

Let's close this chapter by reviewing the four global exponential trends examined thus far. The first trend is Moore's Law, which states that technology is becoming more powerful and less expensive at an increasingly faster pace. The second trend is photonics, which allows data transfer rates per dollar to grow at a rate at least equal and probably exceeding Moore's Law.

These two trends have created a ripple effect and a third global exponential trend: the Internet. On the Internet, everyone is connected to everyone else, and everyone is online, all the time, everywhere. It is a radical shift from text-based information resources to online digital resources. Finally, the intersection of these three global exponential trends has created the Information Age and has led to global exponential trend number four: InfoWhelm. In the very near future, access to the total of all human knowledge will be right in the palm of your hand anywhere, anytime, and within seconds.

Whew! And it doesn't stop there. Respected futurists such as Ray Kurzweil (2005) and James Canton (2006) write that there are more than four global exponential trends—there are probably more like 75 that are quickly coming together into a singularity, the place where man and machine merge.

Summarizing the Main Points

- InfoWhelm is the ever-widening gap between what we understand and what we think we should understand.

- In the age of InfoWhelm, what begins to matter more is not the ability to remember specific content, but rather the ability to place information in a context and use it effectively.

- Today, our data output has exceeded our ability to physically store it.

- Even as Kindle becomes familiar in the mainstream, because of Moore's Law and a device called the iPad, the Kindle may soon become ancient history. Yet, even the iPad is not the end, but a new beginning.

- Despite how our world has changed and continues to change, most of our schools and classrooms continue to operate the way they have for more than 100 years.

- Today, the digital generation is absolutely as comfortable, if not more comfortable, sending and receiving email and text messages, surfing the Web, and reading from a handheld device, cell phone, or computer screen as people of the older generations are reading from a book.

- In the very near future, access to the total of all human knowledge will be in the palm of your hand anywhere, anytime, within seconds.

Some Questions to Consider

- What implications does InfoWhelm hold for you personally and for your family?

- If this has all happened in the past few decades, what do you think might happen in the next decade?

- Once you answer the previous question, consider whether your assumptions are based on linear common sense or exponential thinking. What will the exponential future be?

- What steps can educators take to refocus priorities from 20th-century skills to skills and standards that more accurately reflect the changing realities of the 21st century?

- Does InfoWhelm hold any implications for our schools and the children attending those schools?

- Given that this is a global trend, what skills will children need to have that older generations didn't need to have growing up? What will children need to be able to do with these skills?

- What are we doing in our schools right now to prepare children for a world that will be fundamentally different from the world we grew up in?

Chapter 9
Disruptive Innovation

> Any sufficiently advanced technology is indistinguishable from magic.
>
> **Arthur C. Clarke**

Given what we have laid out to this point, it's easy to predict that what we are looking at for the foreseeable future is continuous and accelerating disruptive innovation. The best way to explain what disruptive innovation means is to give you some examples.

Our great-grandparents had phones that were attached to the wall and came with a crank to make them ring for the attention of the operator. It was connected to a party line, so like it or not, all of your neighbors could listen in on your conversations. Eventually, our grandparents had a phone that sat on a desk or table with a rotary dial and didn't require an operator to dial the number to connect the other party. Over time, the desktop phone became sleeker, and the rotary dial was replaced by push buttons. Cellular phone technology started to emerge in the early 1970s. The first cell phone was affectionately called "the brick" because that's exactly what it looked like. Cell phones in the last few years have progressively become more sophisticated and have become more than just phones. Now, small enough to fit in the palm of your hand, they have the capability to connect to the Internet, to take pictures and movies, to store information (phone numbers, addresses, important dates, and photographs), and to display complex electronic documents or a simple grocery list. Each one of these phones progressively expanded the ways we could communicate with others, and each new generation of the phone was disruptive. Newer phones eventually render the previous versions obsolete.

In the same way, we used to have 33, 45, and 78 rpm records. Do you remember that scratchy sound? Vinyl records eventually gave way to reel-to-reels, then eight-track cartridges, and eventually cassette tapes. Cassette tapes were replaced by CDs and DVDs. Media players, such as iPods and MP3 players, are small, portable, easy to use, and feature large storage capacities, allowing for a variety in the music we can store. They have expanded how and where we could listen to music. Again, at each stage, the newest technologies disrupted and eventually replaced the previous technologies.

The progression of the computer is also a good example of disruptive innovation. In much the same way as telephones and media storage devices, the earliest computers were expensive, complicated, and the size of a building. Twenty years later, they were reduced to the size of a room, but still carried a hefty price tag. Within a decade, a personal computer could reside on a desktop in a person's home or workplace. Within the last decade, computers have become sleeker, faster, and more portable. They are affordable and small enough to fit on your lap or in the palm of your hand. Once again, computer technologies disrupted and eventually replaced the previous technologies.

Now, think about maps. They used to be made of paper and were hard to refold. They were outdated almost from the moment they were printed. For some, they were hard to read and interpret. Today, portable and handheld GPS systems are increasingly popular, and unlike maps, they talk to us and give us driving instructions. This development is particularly great for people who don't want to ask others for directions or admit they're lost. The GPS has changed the way we travel and dramatically increased the amount of information that's instantly at our fingertips, disrupting and in many cases diminishing or eliminating our need for paper maps and bad instructions at gas stations.

And the devices described here are just the very tip of the iceberg. Think of all of the amazing gadgets and devices there are today that didn't exist 5 or 10 years ago—gadgets that allow us to do things that would have been unimaginable even 5 or 10 years ago. As each of these gadgets appeared, they have disrupted the way we work, the way we play, the way we communicate, and the way we think about our fellow citizens.

As each of these gadgets appeared, they have disrupted the way we work, the way we play, the way we communicate, and the way we think about our fellow citizens.

And it's not just gadgets that have been disruptive—it's also the services these gadgets provide that disrupt the way things are done. Woolworth's and then Sears used to be the biggest retailers, but, using computerized data management and distribution systems, Walmart quickly came to dominate the retail world. But increasingly, Walmart has competition from online companies such as Amazon and Best Buy, and thousands of other online retailers have profoundly disrupted traditional retail markets, diminishing and in some cases completely destroying both long-standing traditional companies as well as Mom-and-Pop corner stores.

What about banks? We used to do our banking at a bank Monday through Friday from 10 a.m. to 3 p.m. with a bank teller we knew by name. Not so long ago, the only way you'd get money from a bank on a weekend was with a gun and a mask, or dynamite. Now increasingly we bank using an ATM or a debit or cash card, or we do our banking online 24/7 from our laptop or cell phone. The appearance of ATMs and the emergence of online banking have been hugely disruptive forces that have completely changed our assumptions about how banking is done as well as when and where we can access our accounts.

In the same way, we used to buy and sell things using the classified section of our local newspaper or specialized publications that focused on selling things like cars and boats. Increasingly we use online services like eBay or craigslist. craigslist and eBay have changed buying and selling. They are modern-day yard sales or global digital flea markets that provide online services and have fundamentally changed the relationship between the buyer and the seller. And as before, what has been described here is just the tip of the iceberg.

Everything we have described so far (and many others we haven't profiled) is an example of disruptive innovation. Disruptive innovations have outstripped our capacity to cope, antiquated our laws, transformed our morals, reshuffled our economy, reordered our priorities, redefined our workplace, put our constitution to the fire, and shifted our concept of reality by repeatedly replacing the existing paradigm of life with something new, and when they do, they inevitably reduce the impact and value of what had been the existing paradigm to the point where the previous paradigm no longer dominates the way it once did or it completely disappears.

So What?

The "so what" is that all of these disruptive innovations and many, many, many more just like them have fundamentally and forever changed the way we live life—the way we work, the way we play, the way we communicate, and the way we view our fellow citizens. So let's consider how these disruptive innovations—these disruptive forces—have affected and will affect schools. But to do this, we must first identify a baseline. Schools serve many important services and functions, but let's focus on the question below.

What Are the Mandates of Public Education?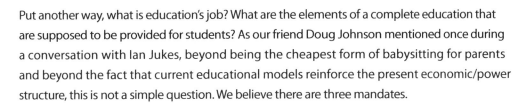

Put another way, what is education's job? What are the elements of a complete education that are supposed to be provided for students? As our friend Doug Johnson mentioned once during a conversation with Ian Jukes, beyond being the cheapest form of babysitting for parents and beyond the fact that current educational models reinforce the present economic/power structure, this is not a simple question. We believe there are three mandates.

The first is the acculturation of the individual. This involves the passing on of the accumulated wisdom of our society through the traditional curriculum—literature, poetry, history, geography, science, mathematics—that are the foundation of the society in which we live.

Second, we strive to cultivate an appreciation of the social, aesthetic, esoteric, philosophical, moral, and ethical. We want to develop students who are socially functional and prepared to operate in the world they're going to live in. We want to help them develop the skills that will make them good people, citizens, parents, community members, and positive contributors to the nation.

Finally (and equally important), we want to help prepare our students to be productive members of society after they leave school: learning to work, working to learn, dealing with the multiple career changes they will experience in their lives; being able to apply 21st-century skills—critical thinking, problem solving, creativity, working in teams, learning in teams, and the ability to use the most appropriate media to solve real-world problems; and taking advantage of every opportunity to develop the skills that will allow them to contribute economically to the nation while ensuring their own financial success.

We might disagree over the language, but hopefully we're on the same page with respect to the contents of this list.

Again, So What?

The problem is that desktop computers and laptops and cell phones and GPS devices and digital cameras and the Internet and online social networking tools like blogs, wikis, podcasts, online video, online shopping, social networking sites, and all the other gadgets and services described here, and many more just like them—not to mention many more that haven't been invented or marketed yet—are all disruptive innovations. And they have created a new digital and information landscape that is driving a world that is fundamentally and exponentially different from the world we grew up in and a future world that will be fundamentally and exponentially different from the world we live in now.

Today, we are all profoundly connected in ways that would have been unimaginable even a few short years ago. We are working, playing, learning and creating together, collaborating, producing, and distributing anytime, anywhere.

This is fundamental change. This is disruptive change. We're confident that many readers are thinking, "Okay, I get it—the world has changed, the way we communicate has changed, and the way we view and interact with others has changed." And once again you may be thinking, so what?

The "so what" is that with disruption there are consequences. The ripple effect is that the way information is distributed has fundamentally and forever changed.

For example, we used to have newspapers and magazines. Now we have Fox, CNN, and Slate. We used to have music stores, and we went to movies. Now we increasingly go to the iTunes store for both our music and movies. We used to have local radio and television; now we have cable, satellite, and Internet radio and TV. We used to have bookstores, and we read paper books. Today we increasingly buy ebooks at Amazon. We used to drive or fly to attend business meetings and conferences. Increasingly we use Skype or iChat or GoToMeeting.com.

We used to meet face-to-face with our banker, stockbroker, accountant, and financial adviser. Now we use an ATM and do our banking, bill paying, and investing online from our kitchen, living room, or bedroom. We used to go to the doctor for medical opinions; now increasingly we go to WebMD or hundreds of other similar services. We used to send handwritten letters and postcards to our friends and family. Now we use email, texting, blogs, Facebook, Twitter, and much more. We used to attend classes at university campuses, local high schools, or community centers. Now we can use Second Life, iTunes University, YouTube.edu, and other virtual learning environments that are doing a great job of serving those kids not well served by traditional schools. Now it will be interesting to see if they drive regular education out the door!

We could go on and on about the many and varied ways that information can be disseminated today, but we think you get the picture. Information is now distributed in fundamentally different ways than it was even 10 short years ago—and, once again, what we have described is merely the tip of the information iceberg.

In the age of InfoWhelm, our world has changed and the way information is distributed and shared has changed, and because we live in exponential times, it will continue to change dramatically, fundamentally, and irrevocably in the next few years. Whether parents, politicians, and educators agree or not, these are highly disruptive times. Every single sector of society that is oriented around information is experiencing a complete upheaval because we are going through an information revolution.

The problem is that our schools and our classrooms are also information organizations, and as educators, educational leaders, and citizens, we have to accept that if the world outside of education is fundamentally transforming and being transformed as a result of disruptive innovation, we can't just pretend that for education and educators it continues to be business as usual in our schools. We can't just pretend that somehow education is immune to the fundamental and disruptive global changes that are occurring outside of education. And we can't assume that we can fix things by tinkering with the existing educational system.

The disruptive forces that are reshaping every other information-oriented sector outside of education in our society are globalizing our economy. What we're seeing is the disappearance of physical, manual labor. According to Levy and Murnane's 2005 book, *The New Division of Labor*, there has been an all-but-complete disappearance of the factory job and factory mindset.

Factory-type jobs were the ones that didn't require a lot of special skills, talent, knowledge, training, or education. You could go down to the factory and get a job, and within a couple of days you could be off and running. And because these jobs didn't require any special training or skills, almost anyone could do them. You didn't even need a high school diploma. You could drop out of school and you could have a well-paying job for life.

What Levy and Murnane tell us is that those jobs are vanishing from the U.S. economy because they can be done by anybody, anywhere. And where labor is cheapest is in the developing world. As we're seeing, that work is quickly being outsourced and off-shored and is disappearing.

We can't just pretend that somehow education is immune to the fundamental and disruptive global changes that are occurring outside of education.

The exceptions are jobs that are location dependent. People who are location dependent include house builders, nurses, plumbers, cab drivers, barbers, auto technicians, restaurant workers, and so on. These workers need to be onsite.

But if a job can be outsourced or sent offshore, it absolutely will be. It's the only way that businesses can stay competitive in an increasingly global economy. Routine cognitive work involves doing the same mental tasks over and over again. We're seeing the disappearance of jobs that involve routine cognitive work. For example, bookkeepers, tax preparers, and receptionists do routine cognitive work. The same goes for people who do data entry, computer programming, legal research, market research, and customer support. Consider people whose jobs involve repetitive mental tasks, such as grocery store cashiers or check-in staff at hotels or airlines, or those who collect highway tolls, process catalog orders, or interpret MRIs and x-rays.

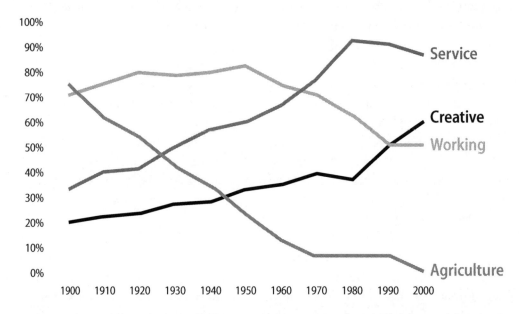

We're seeing this kind of work disappearing primarily because new digital technology can either replace these jobs with computers, machines, and robots or send the work overseas because the cost of workers there is much lower than to employ workers in the United States or Canada. The information needed travels back and forth at the speed of light, whether it's over the phone or over the Internet. Therefore, routine cognitive work can be done anywhere—it's not location dependent.

If you look at what Levy and Murnane say in *The New Division of Labor* (2005), you'll see that the work areas in serious decline are manual work and routine work. Growth areas are in the area of nonroutine cognitive work.

Nonroutine cognitive work is the stuff we refer to as the 21st-century skills. These skills include critical thinking, problem solving, being innovative and creative, being complex communicators, working in teams, and learning in teams. This is the work that can't be replaced by unskilled labor. It can't be replaced by technology or software. It also can't be outsourced to overseas workers.

Every time you make a hotel reservation or purchase an airline ticket over the Internet or drop your mortgage numbers into a web form, you've taken away some frontline routine, cognitive evaluation professional's job. Think about legal software, tax preparation, actuarial work, or purchasing insurance—if it can be reduced to an algorithm, we can produce software that will do it for us. And that segment of the job or the entire job is gone.

But higher-order thinking skills can't be replaced by software. In his book, *The Rise of the Creative Class* (2003), Richard Florida says you can divide American workers into four basic groups. The first group is the agricultural class. In 1900, almost 40 percent of workers were involved in agriculture. In 2010, that's down to less than 2 percent.

The second group is the working class. These are the classic manufacturing jobs that peaked right after World War II and have been in steady decline ever since.

The third group is the service industries or helping professions, which peaked in 1980 and are now steadily shrinking primarily because of the personal computer.

And the fourth group is the creative class. These are the people that do nonroutine cognitive work and apply abstract skills on a regular basis. There's been a sharp upturn in demand for creative class workers since 1980 because of the appearance of the personal computer. Creative class jobs are the jobs that are facilitated by technology, not replaced by it. If you take Florida's line chart and turn it into a bar chart, it looks like this:

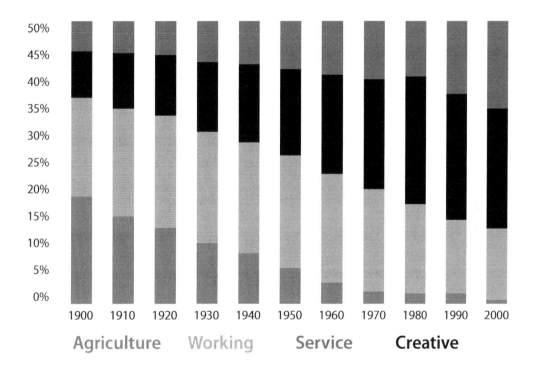

You see a steady decline of agriculture and the steady growth of the creative class. In 1900, only 10 percent of the workforce needed abstract creative cognitive skills. Today that number is estimated to be 35 percent, and this number continues to accelerate primarily driven by digital technologies. The growth areas are in information-oriented professions, business and finance, leisure and hospitality, service providing, and so on.

The declining areas are goods producing, manufacturing, farming, and so on. So to determine the vulnerability or the risk in a particular career or work area, simply ask this question: Can a computer or other disruptive innovation do this job faster? Or can someone overseas do it cheaper than it can be done here? If the answer is yes, that job is gone or will be very shortly. It's just simple economics. That's disruptive innovation!

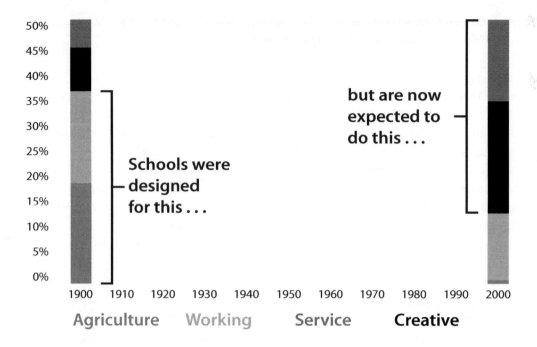

Agriculture   Working   Service   **Creative**

Based on current trends—and there's no reason to doubt that the trends will continue—in 10 years the majority of work in the United States will be creative, nonrepetitive, cognitive work because most of the rest of the work—the work that is routine or that can be done by machines—will be done by lower paid workers overseas in less developed countries or for minimum wage here, or the work will be replaced by software.

 Consider education and, particularly, the three essential mandates we outlined previously:

- To acculturate an individual

- To cultivate an appreciation of the social, aesthetic, esoteric, philosophical, moral, and ethical

- To prepare students to be productive members of society after they leave school

When you look at the data and look at the trends, and when you consider the impact of disruptive innovation, it's very apparent that we have a fundamental problem. Our schools were designed for an era when three quarters of the population were employed in agriculture and manufacturing jobs. But while those times and that world is gone forever, those same educational institutions, those same instructional models, and those same organizational structures are now operating in a world when three-quarters of the workforce is working in creative class and service class professions.

Our current system is continuing to embrace traditional structures, traditional organization, traditional instruction, standardized learning, and standardized tests as the only way to assess learning at the very same time the new economy is eliminating standardized jobs.

Using this mindset, we take kids' uniqueness and shove it into the one-size-fits-all funnel of traditional schools in which we ask students to regurgitate back the "right" answer. In doing so, we try to squeeze square-peg students into round-hole schools. And we use standardized tests and standardized curriculum to define and quantify what it means to be learned in the limitless and ever-changing new digital landscape.

And we are absolutely not being truthful when we assure students and their parents that if they master the state standards they will be prepared for the rest of their lives, and particularly when Bob Marzano's research tells us that about 80 to 85 percent of work that kids do in their classes is factual recall and low-level procedures. In other words, routine cognitive work—the work that is disappearing or being outsourced. And we hear complaints all the time that kids today can't concentrate, that kids can't even memorize the names of the states and their capitals. Meanwhile, the kids are saying, "Why in the world do I have to remember this when I can Google the answer in 3 seconds on my phone?" And many teachers are saying, "What's a Google?"

These same kids, who seem entirely incapable of remembering the names of the states and the capitals, can instantly and with enthusiasm tell you the lyrics of more than a thousand songs or the characteristics of a hundred game characters.

There's no way to sugarcoat it. The bottom line is that the current school system is just not built for the global digital age and the digital generation. Even when you walk into a bright and colorful classroom complete with teacher who has all the students participating and raising their hands, you are being misled because the structural model and operating assumptions of this classroom is exactly the same as it was more than a hundred years ago.

The teacher continues to be the focal point of the room, talking while the students listen; the kids sit in rows and columns; students work individually at their desks. Every once in a while they get to go up and show their work at the front. Structurally, the biggest difference in the classroom from 100 years ago is probably the color of the boards.

As a result, as David Warlick comments, no generation in history has ever been so thoroughly prepared for the Industrial Age. So what is my point?

These are highly disruptive times for education. Education faces multiple disruptive innovations now and in the future. The continued existence of the current educational system is absolutely not certain because the current system was designed to meet a specific needs for a world that increasingly no longer exists, and designed to prepare a massive number of people for an industrial society that is rapidly disappearing.

It is clear that even good organizations with good people and the very best of intentions to do what's right for students run the risk of vanishing if they don't acknowledge and address the relentless nature of disruptive innovation that is replacing an industrial economy with a knowledge economy and replacing the factory worker with a knowledge worker.

As Jack Welch, the former CEO of General Electric, once said, "When the rate of change outside an organization is greater than the rate of change inside an organization, the end is in sight."

Think about all the companies and industries that were once dominant but don't exist anymore. Because of disruptive innovation, they have been replaced by someone or something else. So the message for those inside education is that it's time to change or run the increasing risk of becoming obsolete. And sometimes even change is not enough to save an institution.

The great challenge is that disruptive innovation is a stealth trend. It's sneaking up on most school organizations, and many people inside and outside of education just can't see that this is the case. Many educators continue to think that change is something that happens somewhere else to someone else—that somehow education is immune to the disruptive forces in play outside of education.

If we look at the impact of the transformational technologies and the new digital landscape and consider the new workforce needs for the new competitive global economy, they have, for the most part, existed at the margins of how we operate schools, not at the core.

But we are reaching a tipping point. We are quickly reaching the point where change that is happening on the periphery of our awareness is going to move from being relatively marginal to being massive, sudden, and overwhelming. The bottom line is that we can't just keep pretending this disruptive innovation isn't happening, because it is. That's why we need new schools and, more than that, a new mindset. Economic, technological, informational, demographic, and political forces have transformed and continue to transform the way people live and work. These changes and the rate of change will continue to accelerate. So our schools, like businesses, communities, and families, must constantly adapt to changing conditions to thrive.

That's why we need new schools that will help prepare students for the rest of their lives. We acknowledge that this is hard. The longest journey starts with a single step. The greatest movement starts with a single individual. If it's going to be, it's up to me, it's up to you, it's up to us. Our job is not just to serve what is or has been. Our job is to shape what can, what might, and what absolutely must be.

Summarizing the Main Points

- As new gadgets appeared, they have disrupted the way we work, the way we play, the way we communicate, and the way we think about our fellow citizens.

- Thousands of online retailers have profoundly disrupted traditional retail markets, diminishing and in some cases completely destroying both long-standing traditional companies as well as Mom-and-Pop corner stores.

- Online services have fundamentally changed the relationship between the buyer and the seller.

- We believe there are three mandates for elements of a complete education. The first is the acculturation of the individual. Second, we strive to cultivate an appreciation of the social, aesthetic, esoteric, philosophical, moral, and ethical. Finally, we want to help prepare students to be productive members of society after they leave school.

- Today, we are all profoundly connected in ways that would have been unimaginable even a few short years ago. This is disruptive change.

- We can't just pretend that somehow education is immune to the fundamental and disruptive global changes that occur outside of education.

- The disruptive forces that are reshaping every other information-oriented sector outside of education in our society are globalizing our economy. What we're seeing is the disappearance of physical, manual labor—unless the work is location dependent.

- New digital technology means that routine cognitive work can be done anywhere—it's not location dependent.

- Nonroutine cognitive work is what we call the 21st-century skills. These skills include critical thinking, problem solving, being innovative and creative, being complex communicators, working in teams, and learning in teams.

- The current school system is just not built for the global digital age and the digital generation.

- The message for those inside education is that it's time to change or run the increasing risk of becoming obsolete.

- Schools, like businesses, communities, and families, must constantly adapt to changing conditions to thrive.

- Our job is to shape what can, what might, and what absolutely must be.

Some Questions to Consider

- What are other examples of disruptive innovation in our world today?

- What are examples of technology and services that are commonly available today that didn't exist 25 years ago?

- What jobs or professions have these disruptive forces changed or eliminated?

- Why is there so much change, yet a continued call for change seems to be a constant theme?

- What will you need to know to be able to function in coming ages?

- What have you done to anticipate the future and to identify the land mines you're going to step on that will be driven by technology change?

- Based on what you have just read, brainstorm on the topic of what it will mean to be educated in the 21st century.

- What advice would you give the administration/school board members/ politicians to ensure that the issues of change as outlined in this chapter are addressed appropriately in our schools?

- What strategies do you have for keeping yourself up-to-date on developments in your field of expertise? What magazines, newsletters, online newsgroups, specialty web sites, and other sources exist to help you with this task? Make a list of these informational sources and then develop a plan for butterfly hunting every day. What unexamined assumptions about present schooling do we need to consider?

- What's really critical for our young people to be able to do when their schooling is finished?

- Play out the trends that have been described over the next 10 years. How will they impact our students? What are the implications?

Chapter 10
It's Time for Education to Catch Up

> It is, in fact, nothing short of a miracle that the modern methods of instruction have not yet entirely strangled the holy curiosity of inquiry.
>
> **Albert Einstein**

This Message Is for Everyone

Education is the foundation of our society. We must understand that any society that relies on a highly complex, technological infrastructure that includes highways, railways, airlines, electrical grids, telephones, networks, satellites, and innumerable other high-technology items needs highly competent people to sustain, manage, and develop that society. In the high-technology global market, a nation's ability to compete rests solely on the skill and dedication of its citizens. To be sure, there are many other factors that determine a country's success in the global arena, but if skills and dedication are missing, the rest is insignificant. When these elements are present, they can overcome shortfalls in other areas. So whether we are in business, in education, in government, or retired, we must all see that education is the key to the future. It's everybody's business.

How will the exponential growth of technological power affect education? It is clear that education can't and won't be exempt from the trends we outlined in the previous chapter. The trends we have just discussed will transform learning and education in much the same way as it is transforming the way we work and play. The idea that we can connect to information whenever we need it changes forever the concept of time as it is structured in schools. The ability to learn wherever we are and whenever we need to means distance is no longer a barrier to learning. For the first time in the history of education, the teacher, the student, and the content do not need to be in the same place or even be together at the same time. If time and distance are flexible, and if complete interactive technology allows us to have two- and three-dimensional experiences, what will be left of our current education system? This is an extremely difficult question. In the face of this unbelievable technological upheaval, it's understandable that educators are struggling for answers. Educational institutions know that they must find solutions to this technology dilemma if they are to stay competitive. Still, workable solutions seem elusive. If we can accept the premise that we have been caught with our paradigms down, we will begin to see that part of the solution lies in changing these paradigms and creating new schools and new education structures for the millennium that not only understand but capitalize on the trends just discussed.

Increasingly, we live in a world where change has become the norm. However, many of us grew up in a time where stability was the rule. As we mentioned earlier, change as we knew it then was something very different, something very subtle, something you could measure in terms of years or even decades. Like children growing up, these changes came on us gradually, and we didn't notice them until they were upon us, as measured against last year's growth. Life just isn't like that anymore. The doubling of technological power through the 1990s and early 2000s morphed us into a high-speed, high-tech society. As a result, we are all experiencing accelerated change at a pace never before experienced in human history. Most of us involved in education are simply unprepared for this, and consequently, we have not been able to respond to it as quickly as the world outside education.

We must quickly catch up or face the unenviable prospect of becoming irrelevant. The key to staying relevant is being able to change our focus. As we have discussed, however, to do this we must understand that our attention cannot and must not be placed on the technology itself. Rather, it must be placed on the mindset that guides the use of the new technology coming into schools. Thus, shifting paradigm is paramount. We can't afford to be caught in the backwash as technology races past us. But caught and stuck we are. How could this have happened? Are we truly caught in paradigm paralysis?

Education as a Train

Before we answer this question, let us first picture education as a train. It is pulled by an engine fueled by our desire to educate our children to become effective citizens and to teach them practical skills for success in the world of work. To do this, education must pull many cars down the track—reading, writing, mathematics, geography, history, government, law, languages, science, art, music, woodworking, mechanics, metalworking, and physical education, to name but a few. Today's schools have even more cars being attached to the train in the form of new and different expectations from the public as modern society continues to change.

Now we are being asked to integrate students with special needs, as well as those whose first language is not English. We have become social workers, providing counseling and shelter for students with drug problems or teenage pregnancies. We are asked to watch over those who are victims of physical, emotional, or sexual abuse. We are also asked to take on the role of surrogate parents as families break down. We are expected to build self-esteem, providing personal and moral guidance. All this, while at the same time being responsible for the delivery of a relevant and meaningful academic curriculum. Despite the many obstacles of money, mindset, and time, we are pulling the educational train down the tracks faster and more efficiently than ever before, adding new cars as we go. The truth is that educators today are doing a better job than they ever have.

So, What's the Problem?

Consider the impact technology has had on modern life. Technology has fundamentally and irrevocably changed life for virtually every person in our society. It has compressed time and distance to the point where we can now see history as it happens. World events are viewed in real time, live and uncensored, simulcast on YouTube, Twitter, and email. Mainstream media can't even keep up. Instead of the wire service, they are following the story as it unfolds on the Web. At the same time, an army of volunteer contributors are updating the facts on Wikipedia.

Now consider education in this new high-tech environment. Despite our best efforts, education is increasingly disconnected from the rest of the world we just described. Public education has had very little real competition and, as a result, it has become a virtual monopoly. Educators' responses to the dramatic changes taking place in the outside world are dulled because they approach the changes primarily from an educentric point of view. They tinker with the education system and curriculum as it exists and want to keep it the same instead of addressing what it needs to become for the benefit of the students. They need to ask, "What does a student need to learn?" instead of "What do I want to teach?"

Want proof? Let's compare a classroom in a school to a modern office. Imagine a group of workers who retired 15 years ago returning to their office. What has changed in those years? Everything! Cell phones, voicemail systems, color photocopiers, courier services, the Internet, email, global online collaboration, video conferencing, Facebook marketing, advertising on Twitter, and even the systems and the way of doing business—the list is endless. Businesses have had to invent and reinvent themselves again and again over the course of the past 15 years just to survive. Almost nothing from the old office remains except for perhaps the water cooler.

Now take those same retired workers back to the schools they attended 40 years ago and consider what has changed. While today's school culture and social environment may have changed significantly, from a structural and instructional point of view, very little, if anything, has changed. We still operate in basically the same school day, same school year, same organizational structure, and same instructional delivery model that was used 40 years ago. How can this possibly be?

This is an important question, and the answer reveals much about the nature of the education system. Before we suggest why these retired workers feel so disoriented at work and so comfortable at school, let's summarize what we have said about the nature of modern life. The message has been clear from the outset of the book. Change has become an integral part of our lives. There is no question this is disconcerting for the majority of the population. Anyone over the age of 30 grew up in a much different world than that which exists today. Over the course of the last 15 years, we have moved from the late Industrial Age of stability to the Information and Communication Age of constant and even accelerating change. It's not just about change today and status quo tomorrow—it's about change today, tomorrow, and forever.

Education's Response

How has education responded to this dramatically new technological world we have discussed? The answer is, it hasn't responded in any significant way. The educational system is possibly the most stable institution created by late Industrial Age society. Further, those inside the system have an educentric view of the world that shields them from dealing with the outside world. This sets the stage for a remarkable drama playing out in our schools today.

Returning to our train metaphor, we've just added another car called technology to an already lengthy train. We have put technologically driven change in a compartment so traditional instructional activities can continue untouched. Even though outside of education technology has profoundly affected most of the world we live in, the technology car has not had a parallel effect on any of the other cars on the education train. In many schools today, the use of technology is still considered to be little more than just another add-on. It is not seen as a fundamental and integral aspect of the education train.

While it's true this train is improving, and has even added a modern technology car, it's still a train. It's still basically unaffected by the technological developments of modern life. Unlike the rest of the world, where the power of smart devices is changing the rules of daily life everywhere, education has demonstrated an amazing stability and resistance to such change.

Why? Because many of the people inside the educational system suffer from paradigm paralysis. Like those people we discussed in the first chapter of this book, educators today are victims of their established mindset. This is certainly not to say that they are not intelligent; rather, it's to say that they work in a system increasingly disconnected from the rest of world. Worse, there is little, if any, pressure to connect, let alone keep up, with the rest of the world.

This is due in large part to the fact that much of the evaluation that takes place in the school system is inwardly focused. Educators compare themselves to other educators. Such a perspective promotes the misconception that we are doing the right kind of work with students. This is the real problem facing education today. We are doing a really good job of providing education, but the kind of education we provide is increasingly irrelevant to the modern, changing world in which we live—a world driven by the exponential trends we have presented.

If education is a train, with technology in a separate car, the tracks it runs on are Industrial Age thinking. When microelectronics emerged in the late 1970s, the rest of the world left the track that education was on and took a different path. When technological power continued increasing at a truly astonishing rate in the 1980s, the rest of the world got into an airplane called the Information Age, because a train simply couldn't go as fast or change direction as quickly as one that operates in the freedom of the air.

The rest of the world has changed. We must also change if public education is to survive.

New dimensions, new speeds, and new directions were being developed outside education, but education stayed on its Industrial Age tracks and missed both of these important changes. It continued down the same old track, thinking that it was doing enough by improving the efficiency of the train. The net result was that education became better and better at what it was doing, but at the same time, more and more disconnected and irrelevant to what was happening outside of education.

We must realize that the education system can't continue operating this way. It can't continue to get better at delivering an obsolete education. No matter how much the train is improved, it's still a train. The rest of the world has changed. We must also change if public education is to survive. If we choose to ignore this, private industry will innovate us out of business.

The World in a Rocket

Now we face an even greater challenge. Within the next few years, the rest of the world outside education will be climbing into a rocket and heading for orbit using the new technological devices and powers that started appearing at the beginning of the new millennium. Why a rocket? And why so quickly? Didn't the world just switch from a train to an airplane?

The answer lies with the trends we discussed earlier. Many educators do not yet fully appreciate that the technology they see and use is just part of a continuum of developing technological power. While we were busy with the details of our normal lives, electronic technology has steadily doubled in power time and again over the last 50 years.

However, the real story is what lies ahead. As the saying goes, "You ain't seen nothin' yet!" As we have presented, the exponential growth in technological power is about to kick into overdrive in much the same way it did for the farmer who asked his king for grains of wheat. For the farmer, the result was an unbelievable payday when the king reached the end of the chessboard. For us, the result will be some truly unbelievable technologies. None of us are prepared for what is about to unfold. However, unlike the situation with the farmer, the doubling effect of technological power does not stop at the end of the chessboard. This story of developing technological power will extend well into the 21st century, with no foreseeable end. We are about to get into a rocket, technologically speaking.

What will this doubling effect have on our lives? Although it's difficult to accurately predict exactly what the technology will look like, there is little doubt that it will revolutionize virtually every aspect of human endeavor.

What about education? Let's consider the children who are entering the school system in kindergarten right now. What kind of world will they graduate into? What should the school system be doing now to prepare them for that future? With changes of such enormous magnitude coming within such a short time frame, we can't continue to just tinker with a train that needs a complete overhaul. In fact, it may be time to discard the train. This is because fundamental and pervasive changes are required if we want education to survive, let alone be relevant, in the world of the 21st century.

Many educators know something big is happening in the world outside education today. Many even say they want a new system to meet the changing needs of the students who will live in the world of tomorrow. Still, they continue to act in the same way that they have for years. However, rhetoric is not the language of change. In and of itself, it can't transform education.

If a new system is what's needed, we must begin to do things differently. The changes we must make to the way we prepare students for the rest of their lives must be substantial. True, we won't be able to make these changes overnight, but change we must. These changes will take some time, so we need to get moving today. If education hopes to meet the challenge of preparing the students of today for the world of tomorrow, it must break out of its current mindset and move ahead rapidly to embrace the new paradigm of constant and accelerating change.

Summarizing the Main Points

- Education is the key to the future—and it's everybody's business.

- The ability to learn wherever we are and whenever we need to means distance is no longer a barrier to learning.

- As a result of becoming a high-speed, high-tech society, we are all experiencing accelerated change at a pace never before experienced in human history.

- Public education has become a virtual monopoly, which has dulled many educators to the need to respond to the changes taking place in the outside world.

- We are doing a really good job of providing education, but the kind of education we provide is increasingly irrelevant to the modern, changing world in which we live.

Some Questions to Consider

- Why are schools still using the same instructional delivery model that was used 40 years ago?

- Why do many of the people inside the educational system suffer from paradigm paralysis?

- How has education become more and more disconnected and irrelevant to what is happening outside of the classroom?

- What has changed in education over the past 40 years?

- What changes must be made to the educational system to prepare students for the future?

Jenny and the High-Tech School of the Future

A typical day in the life of a digital student

After waiting for 10 minutes on a cold winter morning, Jenny finally gets on the school bus and sits at the back. She takes her minicomputer out of her backpack and begins to do some work since the bus is equipped with a wireless high-speed connection. The computer is the size of a comic book, and she controls the device by speaking to it and by touch. She checks her email and then she has a short video chat with her dad at work to ask if she can order pizza with her friends after the game.

The school bus was late in arriving to the school, so Jenny goes directly to her first class. After waving her microchip student card at the card reader, which automatically records her attendance, Jenny sits down and takes out her minicomputer. She positions it so the camera captures what the teacher is doing. She has found it very helpful to record her math classes because the teacher often goes too fast for her to keep up. Viewing parts of a lesson again has helped Jenny to bring her grade up considerably.

Jenny's math teacher uses an electronic board to display his teaching. He sits casually on the front of his desk with a small tablet in his hands. Using a pen-shaped stylus, he writes his math examples on the tablet. His work is displayed on a large electronic board on the wall behind him. The system automatically creates perfect circles, ellipses, parabolas, hyperbolas, and so on. Students walk up to the board and manipulate the formulas and graphs by using their fingers on the board. Her teacher sends the work he is doing to the students' computer tablets and allows them to work on the math problems independently or as a group.

When the bell rings, Jenny goes to her locker to hang up her coat and drop off her backpack. Then, she goes to her virtual Spanish class. Jenny practices her Spanish pronunciation by speaking into her computer. The software on her computer gives her feedback on how she is pronouncing the words. It also translates English into Spanish so she can hear how sentences are constructed as well as learn the Spanish vocabulary for English words. Halfway through the period, Jenny's Spanish teacher appears on her screen. Mr. Buscaglia has found that recording his lessons and sending them out to the students' computers allows him to get the attention of all the students, and they can also review what he is saying for future reference. Today, he asks the students to work in groups of three to film the interaction between a salesperson and customers asking for assistance in buying a pair of jeans—in Spanish, of course.

At the end the period, Jenny heads back to her locker to pick up her lunch. Then, she goes to the cafeteria to have lunch with her friends. After eating, she talks with her friends and conducts several simultaneous text and video chat conversations with other friends on her cell phone. Some of her friends are in other locations in the school, and others are at various places around town.

At the end of lunch break, Jenny heads to her Social Studies class. She is working on a video presentation about World War II. It is a collaborative project, and her partners are students in Spain. Her homework last night involved a videoconference with her partners in Madrid, two students in her same year. Jenny was able to practice her Spanish while Alejandro and Clàudia worked on their English. They worked on the video collaboratively, sharing photos and music they each had assembled and built into the project in real time.

Jenny opens the video and reviews it with other students in her class, whose role is to assess if the project is meeting the assignment criteria. While their teacher supervises, they offer suggestions to make it better and check off the points that have been addressed. She works on the edits and then posts an update and records a video explanation of what she's done for Alejandro and Clàudia.

When they are done, Jenny heads to the student lounge to get ready for her online Biology class. She sees that the next unit in the course is cell division. She begins her studies on this material by going to Second Life to listen to a lecture on cell division. Then she goes to the resources section of the system and views an online simulation of meiosis and mitosis to compare and contrast the differences between these two methods of cell division. She has a couple of questions about what she has seen, so she contacts an online tutor and has a video chat session with her to get clarification on the differences in the two types of cell division she has encountered.

When Jenny finishes her Biology work, she downloads a video from the library about World War II to watch while she waits for her basketball game to start. After the game, she uses her cell phone to order from the pizza web site and arranges the delivery time for when she'll get back with her friends.

On her way home, she receives a video call from Alejandro and Clàudia, who really like her changes to the video and are putting the finishing touches on it. They let her know it will be uploaded to the class portfolio for streaming tonight and ready for her to deliver the presentation tomorrow as planned.

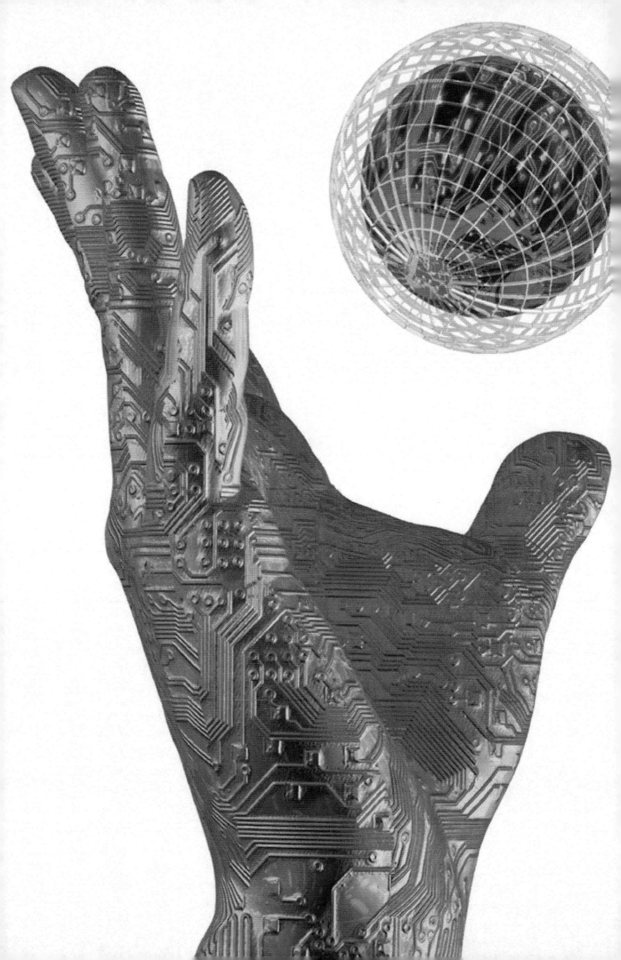

Chapter 11
Education in the Future

> **If you don't know where you're going, you'll probably end up somewhere else.**
>
> **Yogi Berra**

You just read the story of Jenny and the High-Tech School of the Future. Although it sounds futuristic, the truth is that all of those things are possible and are being done today. It only seems like the future because of how mired in the past our traditional approach to instruction is. In education, our focus is on the short term, preparing kids for the next unit, the next semester, or the next grade. In doing so, we are missing the fact that the changes we've described up to this point are making our current system obsolete.

The key to making successful change is knowing where we are going. Without a clear goal in mind, much effort may be wasted in heading in the wrong direction. The first thing we must do is to establish a goal or target to aim for. How do we determine what our goal should be, particularly in light of the rapidly changing modern world? To begin, there is a basic rule to follow. We should never limit our focus by only looking at what's "hot" today. In times of exponential change, we can't base our decisions just on what exists. Rather, as we have discussed, what exists today can only be fully understood when seen as part of a continuum that stretches into the future. The world of technology is changing so quickly that many companies have adopted a corporate motto: "Today let's put ourselves out of business, because if we don't, someone else will!" We would do well to adopt a similar motto in education, not just because the world is changing but also because our mandate is to prepare our students for their lives in the future. The only way to adequately plan for the future is to look at the big picture that started in the past and moves through the present and into the future.

We must look at education the same way that the quarterback looks at the football field. We must perceive where things are headed so we can respond appropriately. This will require us to apply all that we have discussed in this book. We must accept that we have a paradigm for how we expect life to unfold. We must accept that in times of radical change, we all suffer from some degree of paradigm paralysis. We must accept that change requires us to let go of ideas and ways of doing things that we hold dear. Keep this in mind as we outline the future goals for education. We need to shift our focus again and take the trends that are running through the present into the future and re-aim our sights. What we see is a shift from education with all of its connotations of the school system, brick-and-mortar classroom, teachers lecturing, textbooks, worksheets, standardized tests, bells—in fact, everything we grew to up expecting school to be—to learning whenever and wherever it can best happen.

1. Learning Is Customized for the Learner

Learning has never been a problem—young children learn intuitively. Learning in school, however, has been quite a different matter. The problem is that the school system is designed more for handing large numbers of young people than it is designed for individual students. Currently economics, paradigm, and pragmatics limit instruction to an approximately 30-to-1 ratio of students to teacher. Our entire system of schools, systems, and tests are created around this 30-to-1 approach to instruction, and that necessitates teaching to a group rather than teaching individually. Individual needs and interests are sacrificed in the name of expediency. Students are grouped by classes, grades, and geography because considering other factors is just too complicated for most school districts. But this has a real cost in terms of meeting the needs of all the students in any of these groupings. For example, in a typical group of 30 students, there is a wide range of abilities, interests, maturity, and learning styles. To reach the largest number of students and for the sheer sanity of the teacher, he or she has to teach to the middle in terms of student ability. Given the current model and assumptions on which education operates, while customization is a laudable goal, it is unrealistic.

The major casualty in this approach is engagement for the individual student. This is a problem of immense proportions because any teacher will tell you that engagement is the key ingredient to real learning. By not addressing the individual abilities and interests of each student, we have created an educational system that works against our ultimate goal of fostering a love for learning in each of the students in our charge. In fact, the design of the current system goes against what we know about learning from brain research. Listen very closely to what John Medina has to say in his book, *Brain Rules*:

> *Every student's brain . . . is wired differently. That's the* Brain Rule. *You can either accede to it or ignore it. The current system of education chooses the latter, to our detriment. It needs to be torn down and newly envisioned, in a Manhattan Project-size commitment to individualizing instruction. We might, among other things, dismantle altogether grade structures based on age.* (Medina, 2008, p. 69)

But now, based on the emergence of the new technologies that we have discussed and the trends that are moving through the present into the future, we can easily see that technology will soon be able to empower us to achieve our ultimate goal of individualized instruction for the school system. Technology will soon have the power to adjust the delivery of course content to the individual abilities of students. When this occurs, there will be a major shift in the focus of schooling away from achievement based on age and grade level to a focus on the mastery of content and skills. Technology will empower individual students to master course material at their own pace.

Technology will also empower students to accomplish learning tasks when and where it is convenient or practical for a particular student. Parents and teachers can tell you that many teenagers' biorhythms make them want to stay up until 3 a.m. and sleep until the early afternoon. This is a problem when schools start classes at 8:30 a.m. But with electronic computer and telecommunication systems that are always on and always ready to respond, technology will allow students to connect with learning resources whenever it works for them. When you consider where the power of wired and wireless communication is today and where it is heading, it is easy to predict that very fast connections to the global digital network will soon be ubiquitous. When this is combined with the staggering growth in the capabilities of technology to handle all types of information, this has huge implications for where learning will take place. No longer will education be confined to school buildings. It will take place in parks, on buses, in homes, on boats, in museums, in city halls, in zoos, on football fields, on hiking trails, beside streams, at the ocean shore, and so on. Learning will take place almost anywhere the student has a teachable moment. This will not replace traditional learning, but rather augment it to make learning more relevant.

2. Learning Is Nonlinear

New technologies will not only facilitate the pursuit of individual interests, they will keep track of individual progress through established educational milestones in a nonlinear fashion. This is impractical in the education system that is currently in place. Students are forced into classes where concepts are taught in a unit-by-unit sequence, year after year. Teachers cannot keep track of students who do not follow the established path through the course content. One of the authors can remember being hit on the hand with a ruler (yes, teachers actually did that kind of thing to students in the 1960s) for reading chapter six in his science textbook when the rest of the class was still reading chapter five.

Real learning often follows a nonlinear path that develops as cognitive links are formed. For example, a student who reads the novel *1984* may become intrigued with ideas of the future and quickly move on to Ray Bradbury's book, *Fahrenheit 451*. Or a 6th-grade student may become interested in rockets and pursue the topic further and find ideas from the 8th-grade science curriculum, 10th-grade science curriculum, and 12th-grade or college physics curriculum. The wonderful thing about this kind of learning is that, because interest drives the learning, it will be more complete and long lasting than if the student had been forced to consider science six concepts before science seven and science eight, each separated by a calendar year. This kind of learning spawns engagement because it allows students to follow spontaneous ideas and interests. David Thornburg captured the power of this kind of learning during a presentation at a CUE California Conference in 1995:

> *Technology allows learners to move through conceptual space at the speed of thought.* (1995)

The real problem with this kind of learning is that it has been impossible to keep track of an individual's progress. However, exponential growth in the power of technology will soon produce intelligent technology to easily keep track of the path these conceptual links follow for each individual student. How is this possible? Let's look at an example from Amazon.com. Amazon. com uses a technology called System for Managing Agents in Real Time (SMART Agents), which learns about a person's interests from their purchasing history and then makes suggestions for what he or she might be interested in next. Intelligent tracking software would guide students as they progress on their journey of developing cognitive links. This technology would offer helpful suggestions to students that they can explore to further develop their interest in an area, as well as meet their curricular goals.

Nonlinear learning will significantly change the way we look at student progress. The whole notion of grade groupings and sequential course material will be abandoned. It is possible for a 13-year-old student to meet some of the instructional goals for the English curriculum for English 9, 10, 11, and 12 in a two-week period and the system will keep track of his or her progress. Intelligent tracking software will ensure that all instructional holes are filled by reminding students of curricular goals that have not yet been met and directing the student to learning experiences that will cover the required course content. We have no problem in seeing that some instructional goals for Grade 7, for example, may not be met until a student is 16 years old, while at the same time that student may have achieved mastery of English concepts presented up to the third-year college level. This is a shift that has been anticipated since 1959 when J. Lloyd Trump foresaw this kind of freedom in his book, *Images of the Future.*

3. Learning Is Both Virtual and Physical

Technology has already made virtual relationships part of our lives. It started with the telephone and has progressed into communicating via email, online chatting, and video conferencing with programs like Skype. We are also beginning to see the appearance of three-dimensional virtual worlds in computer games and online sites like Second Life. While they are still somewhat crude and limited by the two-dimensional screen, they have already become hugely popular and point to new virtual worlds when viewed from an exponential perspective.

It is easy to see that these 3-D virtual worlds will blur the lines between real life and virtual reality in the near future. Virtual worlds will become more and more realistic. They will allow people to interact in virtual 3-D space. The virtual figures that you will interact with will become more and more lifelike. Virtual communication with people from around the world will approach the ease of real-world communications.

This will have profound implications for education. Virtual relationships will become commonplace. Teachers and students will no longer have to be in the same place for learning to occur. But more important, the quality of the interaction between the virtual teacher and the virtual students will be sufficiently natural that the communication will not suffer simply because they are not face to face. This will be a real shock to those educators who grew up and entered the teaching profession with a brick-and-mortar mentality for what schools look like and where learning takes place. The advantages of this kind of interaction will make its use compelling in the learning endeavor in the near future.

The virtual component of learning will not be limited just to communication. Dedicated virtual learning environments will be constructed to teach students about the world. In the not too distant future, simulations will allow students to shrink down in size and see the unseen world of the very, very small, to break free of the constraints of the earth and explore the universe, and to select a wide range of learning experiences in between these two extremes that seem only in the realm of science fiction today.

But school should still be a physical place because learners will still need to work on their interpersonal skills. In fact, as virtual relationships and learning experiences become more common, well-rounded individuals must have social skills to fully function in the world. In the future, many students will go to school and experience physical interaction in smaller, community-based schools that are close to their homes. Students will still be able to meet, discuss, play basketball, and interact with other students and adult teachers, but the need for a large school building with all its resources will be greatly diminished due to access to virtual learning resources.

4. Learning Is Assisted by Thinking Machines

A long-standing goal in technological development has been a completely natural interaction with machines capable of thinking independently, like the robots and androids you see in *Star Wars* or *Star Trek*. Up until now, electronic technology has not yet provided the general public with anything that approaches the *Star Wars* droid level of intelligence. What it has provided are powerful tools for searching, retrieving, viewing, organizing, calculating, and editing information. These tools have helped us accomplish many tasks that would normally be beyond human capabilities. However, as powerful as these tools are, their use has been guided by direct human involvement. High-level thinking and the decision-making process have been exclusively human tasks.

But we are seeing the beginning of a new era of intelligent machines running software that is capable of exercising independent, high-level, decision-making skills and interaction. As we mentioned earlier, Amazon.com's SMART Agent suggests new purchases based on information it stores about a buyer's previous purchases. Voice recognition software is being installed into new cars to allow for hands-free telephones, radios, and GPS equipment. Some new models have a hands-free parallel park feature where the car will literally park itself. These developments are impressive, but when they are viewed with an understanding of the exponential growth in the power of technology, it is easy to predict the widespread use of thinking machines in the near future. In his book, *The Extreme Future*, James Canton (2006) makes the following statement regarding the exponential growth in the power of machines:

> With decreased costs of computer chips and vast, exponential increases in processing power, all products in the future will have the capacity to "think." Products will be connected and sense, talk, interact, and make decisions with humans and for humans. (Canton, 2006, p. 256)

We must embrace the idea that intelligent machines will soon become a part of everyday life. This will have a major influence on the workplace and education. Students will be able to interact with smart tutors that will assist them with skill development in mathematics and reading. Online sites will run intelligent software that will present learning material to students in a variety of formats and respond to student questions. In addition, this smart software will be able to learn from experience and then tailor instruction to the individual learning style of a particular student. Face recognition will enable the software to respond to the individual student automatically with complete knowledge of his or her learning history and preferences. Interacting with this intelligent software either online or embodied in a robot or car will become as natural as interacting with human teachers.

This will greatly alter the role of teachers in learning. No longer will they be burdened with the delivery of course content, but instead will be free to work on high-level instructional tasks. This will be accomplished by smart learning agents both in the classroom and online.

5. Learning Is Focused on Processing Multimedia Information

In his book, *Mind Set!*, John Naisbitt (2006) makes a very simple statement that has huge significance for educators:

> *A visual culture is taking over the world.* (Naisbitt, 2006, p. 113)

The statement is startling. Most educators, both those currently teaching or administrating or those still in training, are products of an education system focused on processing textual information. Even though the world around us is changing radically, educators are still married to words. While there are substantial reasons for continuing to teach students to read, write, and process words, our connection with the daily reality of the modern world is tenuous because we have not embraced the growing visual culture that students, parents, consumers, and businesspeople experience through the print and electronic media. Naisbitt's statement is a wake-up call to those currently involved in education.

However, when Naisbitt's statement is viewed from the perspective of exponential growth and a world of "InfoWhelm," it is clear that audio/visual communication through a variety of media will become the norm in a few short years. Equipping students with the skills required to process multimedia messages will very soon become imperative, if it is not already the case.

Education in the future will focus on two sets of multimedia information processing skills. The first set of skills will be concerned with how a student receives and decodes messages sent in a wide range of media formats. Can the student see the real message being communicated? Is there bias in the information being presented? The second set of skills involves the communication of messages by the student using various multimedia formats. Students are not only consumers of information in the modern world, they are also producers and publishers of information. Students will need to learn how various media can be manipulated to better communicate what they want to say. They must learn the underlying principles of the use of color and graphic design as well as the principles of video and sound production if they are going to be masters of this new multimedia environment.

6. Learning Is Collaborative

Collaboration is now a driving force in the world. Individuals collaborate in networked games to accomplish tasks, students from different parts of the world are beginning to cooperate on projects for school, workers routinely cooperate with coworkers using a variety of online tools, and even businesses that compete with one another are discovering that working together is the best strategy for success. The power of this transformation in thinking is captured by Tapscott and Williams (2006) in their book, *Wikinomics*.

> *Indeed, as a growing number of firms see the benefits of mass collaboration, this new way of organizing will eventually displace the traditional corporate structures as the economy's primary engine of wealth creation.* (Tapscott & Williams, 2006, p. 1)

Collaboration is quickly becoming an essential strategy for success in the 21st century for individuals, workers, and companies. Consequently, collaboration skills will become essential life skills for students to acquire in school as they prepare for the modern workplace. We are not talking about the skills that students learn when they are put in groups of two or three in a classroom. While this kind of collaboration is a good beginning, students must progress into activities that involve working with people who are not physically present. Students will have to become at ease working with virtual partners and how to function in a workgroup separated by time and distance.

Collaboration will also happen with instruction. Teachers will not have to be the only expert in the classroom. New online tools will allow students to meet with experts in various fields who can assist with the teaching of course content. These tools will also allow experts to come into the school environment virtually to help with instruction. The responsibility for learning will become shared between educators and the community.

7. Learning Is Whole Mind

Education in the future will shift away from the current focus on tasks that predominantly use only the left side of the brain to tasks that exercise both sides of the brain at once. To grasp the significance of this shift, let's briefly examine how the brain works. Brain research has revealed that there are two hemispheres in our brains that have quite different functions. The left hemisphere of the brain handles those things that are sequential in nature—reading, writing, and arithmetic, for example. It also deals with the literalness of words and events. The left side of the brain handles logical reasoning. It wants to break images and events down into their components because analysis is what it does best.

The right hemisphere of the brain is quite different from the left. It has the ability to deal with more than one thing simultaneously. In so doing, the right side of the brain can see things in context and resolve contradiction to determine the meaning of situations. The right side also handles emotion and is largely responsible for creative activities like painting, playing music, and imagining stories. The right brain wants to see all the components of images and event simultaneously because synthesis is what it does best. As a result, the right brain helps us see the big picture in what happens around us.

Brain research has further discovered that high-level thought involved in solving complex problems always involves both sides of the brain working in concert. This is an important point that will have significant implications for education in the future. Traditionally, school has focused on activities that exercise the left side of the brain—reading, writing, arithmetic, and logical analysis. This approach served people well in the late Industrial Age of the 20th century.

However, the emergence of the Information Age as a result of technological development has changed the kinds of skills that people need for success in the world. Consider this quote from David Brooks (2008), a writer for *The New York Times*:

> *Employers now require fewer but more highly skilled workers. The central process driving this is . . . the skills revolution. We're moving into a more demanding cognitive age. In order to thrive, people are compelled to become better at absorbing, processing and combining information.* (Brooks, 2008)

This new age of automation and outsourcing are forcing workers to develop their higher-level thinking skills. It is important to note that being able to process information to see patterns, make connections, determine meaning, and see the big picture are right-brain tasks. While students still must develop left-brain skills in reading, writing, doing arithmetic, and performing logical analysis, they must also develop their right-brain skills in information processing and problem solving. The importance of this shift is captured in this terrific quote from Daniel Pink (2006) in his book, *A Whole New Mind*:

> *In a world tossed by Abundance, Asia, and Automation, in which left-brain-directed thinking remains necessary but no longer sufficient. . . . We must perform work that overseas knowledge workers can't do cheaper, that computers can't do faster, and that satisfies the aesthetic, emotional, and spiritual demands of a prosperous time.* (Pink, 2006, p. 61)

Education in the future will make a significant shift toward valuing learning tasks that exercise both the left and the right sides of the brain at the same time. These whole-mind tasks will look surprising to many teachers used to the left-brain tasks of 20th-century education. Students will spend time drawing, painting, playing music, and doing creative writing because these activities exercise both sides of the brain. Already businesses are discovering that people who have developed their creative skills are better at coming up with solutions to business problems. This shift to whole-mind teaching will be a hallmark of education in the future.

8. Learning Is Based on Discovery

Teachers talk, students listen—repeatedly, day in and day out. Students read textbooks and take notes. Then students cram for tests and try to memorize as much of the content that has been presented to get a good grade as they can. This is the essential paradigm of 20th-century education. The problem is that this is an incredibly ineffective way for students to learn anything at all.

> *Most of the content students get is dismissed as soon as they graduate (or pass the test).* (The Buck Institute for Education, 2003, p. 154)

The grim reality is that most students have forgotten the content they memorized within 48 hours after the test. Worse yet, with this learning process students do not develop any skills that will be useful to them outside the walls of school. The reason teachers teach this way is because they feel the pressure to cover a curriculum in an arbitrary 8- to 10-month period of time. Teachers must prepare students to be promoted to the next grade the following school year. While most teachers would prefer to take more time to delve deeper into the material in their courses, the limits of time to fulfill all standard requirements prevent them from exploring alternative methods of instruction.

But because of the exponential growth in technological power, this will soon change. Teachers will be empowered to treat students as individuals. Earlier, we mentioned that progress through course material will be freed from the arbitrary constraints of today to allow students to progress at their own pace and to follow nonlinear paths through course content. Students will discover new information, ideas, and concepts. The learning they do will have more influence and long-lasting results.

Discovery learning is a trend that has started occurring in the world today. It's not happening in schools yet, but it's happening as young people search the Internet for information on topics that interest them. They are getting online lessons to learn how to play the guitar, searching Google for advice on how to fix a mountain bike or the alternator on their car, checking Facebook or blogs for what their favorite movie star or music group is doing, learning how to alter images in Photoshop through YouTube, and investigating what to do about an annoying skin rash from WebMD. They are discovering all kinds of things about the world around them—just not the kinds of things they encounter at school.

In the future, exponential growth in the power of technology will produce online sites with SMART Agents that will present multimedia information to students in natural interactions involving voice, facial expression, and body language. Simulations will empower students to discover how the world around them works through amazingly realistic virtual experiences of the microscopic, the world of outer space, and everything in between. History will come alive with re-creations of important events, battles, conferences, speeches, and so on. Students will have access to information sources that will allow them to experience current events firsthand as they happen. Learning will shift from secondhand experiences through lectures and books to firsthand discovery experiences. Teachers will no longer be saddled with the burden of being the primary source of instruction. Instead, their focus will shift to creating learning tasks that challenge their students to develop higher-level thinking skills.

9. Teaching Is About Crafting Problems

As we have mentioned, how a teacher delivers the content of a course to students is a long-standing approach to teaching. But as technology increases in power, teachers will be able to devote their time to creating the kinds of learning activities and projects that will foster high-level thinking for their students. These are the thinking skills that workers will need for success in the future because technology will take over most of the low-level thinking tasks that people do today. We are already seeing the replacement of low-level thinking tasks in the workplace. Teachers and students alike will be able to focus on assessing various sources of information, looking for patterns, making connections between the data collected from different sources, and sorting out extraneous or incorrect information in order to see the big picture in material retrieved from their research—then solving problems, creating new products, or performing useful work by applying that newfound knowledge.

A key role for teachers in the future will be to take the material in courses such as English, science, social studies, and mathematics and craft problems for students to solve that will lead them into the required content while forcing them to develop high-level thinking skills as they perform the task. This kind of thinking and skill development will serve them well when they graduate from school. The growing importance of teachers making the shift to problem-based instruction will require a reeducation of teachers, especially those who have taught using a traditional 20th-century approach. This reeducation will go further than just learning how to craft problems from course material. The kinds of activities that students will do to prepare them for the workplace of the future will change radically due to the shift in importance of right-brain thinking. Consider this quote from Daniel Pink (2006):

> Left-brain-directed aptitudes—the sorts of things measured by the SAT and deployed by CPAs—are still necessary. But they're no longer sufficient. Instead, the right-brain-directed aptitudes so often disdained and dismissed—artistry, empathy, taking the long view, pursuing the transcendent—will increasingly determine who soars and who stumbles. It's a dizzying—but ultimately inspiring—change. (Pink, 2006, p. 27)

Teachers of traditional academic subjects will have to embrace the use of right-brain thinking activities as vehicles for teaching their students. Students in mathematics could be solving problems involving the playing of musical instruments. Students in science could use paintings to illustrate concepts in chemistry. Students in social studies could write creative fictional stories based on historical figures and events. These kinds of tasks will not only cover course content, but they will also help students to develop the whole-mind thinking skills they will need for future success.

10. Evaluation Is Holistic

The main evaluative tool used by the school system for measuring student performance is the written test. Of those tests, many are multiple-choice format because they are easy to check for accuracy, either by the teacher or by an optical card reader. These evaluative tools give teachers a snapshot of what a student knows about specific details on a certain topic. The question is, do these tools give a complete and accurate picture of student learning?

To understand the scope of what written tests reveal about a student's learning, let's think about how the motor vehicle department decides whether a person has learned enough to be allowed to drive a car on public roads. Student drivers must learn the rules of the road and some basic concepts of speed and braking before they are allowed a learner's permit. Ensuring that this information has been learned is evaluated with a multiple-choice test. But that only gets you a learner's permit to practice driving a car. The final evaluation is done by an examiner who rides along with the student driver to gauge the level of driving skill as the student performs various driving tasks. Although the aptitude test is one part of the evaluation, it could not measure the level of skill a student has in driving, stopping, and parking the car.

It is easy to see that written tests have a part to play in evaluation. However, it is only a small part. Tests can't give a complete picture of what a student has learned from his or her schooling experience. Skills developed in solving problems, creating videos, drawing pictures, playing an instrument, refuting an argument in a debate, building a desk, cooking a meal, playing basketball, and a whole host of other skills are missed if written tests are the main evaluative tool. The narrow scope of what tests measure is a source for considerable frustration for both students and teachers in the current approach used by our school system.

Teachers are already overburdened with onerous demands on their time. Asking them to consider a more holistic evaluation of student learning, while desirable, is simply not practical. However, when the exponential growth in technological power is factored in, evaluation may be taken over by sophisticated software in the near future. As this occurs, teachers will have time to focus on those aspects of evaluation that are currently underused or not used at all. This will be an important shift because many of the skills and attributes of people who will be successful in the future are not easily measured by written tests.

Summarizing the Main Points

- What exists today can only be fully understood when seen as part of a continuum that stretches into the future.

- Customization and individualization of education is unrealistic with today's current model.

- As virtual relationships and learning experiences become more common, individuals must have social skills to fully function in the world.

- Intelligent machines will soon become a part of daily life, and this will have a major influence on the workplace and education.

- Education in the future will experience a shift from primarily left-brain skills to whole-mind tasks.

- Collaboration is an essential strategy for success in the 21st century.

- Written tests have a part to play in evaluation; however, tests can't give a complete picture of what students have learned from their schooling experience.

Some Questions to Consider

- What are the future goals for education?

- What knowledge have we gained about learning from brain research?

- What implications will virtual communication and learning environments have for education?

- What is the importance of the two sets of multimedia information processing skills necessary for education in the future?

- How will education in the future be influenced by discovery learning?

- Why is teacher reeducation important as education makes the shift to problem-based instruction?

solution
fluency

information
fluency

creativity
fluency

digital citizen

media
fluency

collaboration
fluency

Chapter 12
New Skills for a New World

> By failing to prepare, you are preparing to fail.
>
> **Benjamin Franklin**

"What are they teaching these kids?" asked the owner of a local coffee shop. He then went on to tell a story. Like most of his employees, Jesse was a high school student preparing to go to college in a few months. He would be graduating at the top of his class.

Early one Saturday morning the owner's phone rang at his home. It was Jesse calling. "We're out of milk, so I've closed the coffee shop," Jesse said.

Horrified at the prospect of the lost revenue on the busiest day of the week, the owner (now wide awake) said, "Check the fridge, I know there are several gallons in there. Another delivery arrives in a few hours. You'll be fine."

Jesse replied, "But those are all skim milk and we need whole milk to make lattes." The owner sighed. "You have whipping cream and you have skim milk. Just make whole milk from them to get you by, all right?"

"Oh sure … I guess," Jesse replied. "Um, actually, I have no idea how to do that. Can you tell me what to do?" asked Jesse.

"It's really simple. Whole milk is 3.25 percent milk fat. Skim milk is 0 percent milk fat and whipping cream is 32 percent milk fat. Just mix the whipping cream and skim milk in a 10:1 ratio," said the owner.

"Wow, I never would have thought of that!" said Jesse.

"But don't they teach you how to solve problems in school?" asked the owner.

"Not really." replied Jesse. "We don't really get the chance to figure things out. They show us how it's done and then we just repeat it. Oh, hey. Kalina will be here in an hour. If we run out again I'll go to the 7-Eleven to get more."

"Now you're thinking!" said the owner.

How can this be? How can a bright kid like Jesse do so well in school and not be able to solve this problem on his own? It's because we don't focus on <u>critical thinking and problem-solving</u> skills in school. We pose a problem, and then give students the solution.

We give them the product of our thinking and don't challenge them to discover learning on their own. If we did, an honor student like Jesse would be able to figure out how to mix the milk. Better still, as the owner pointed out later, there was money in the cash register and a convenience store on the corner. Jesse or one of the other employees could have bought a few gallons of whole milk to get them through for a few hours until the order arrived. Instead, Jesse's solution to the problem was to close the coffee shop.

Highly achieving students have developed special abilities that allow them to move smoothly through the school system. They develop the necessary skills to effectively cram for and write tests. What the most academically successful students have learned to do well is to play the game called school. Although they can perform brilliantly in school, they do not function well in life beyond the written test.

Their school skills do not include the necessary high-level critical thinking skills and competencies that are needed to live and work in the real world beyond the school, solving real-world, real-life problems in real time. Somewhere, we have lost sight of the need for our students to become independent thinkers and doers. Instead, in our efforts to ensure compliance in our learners, we have developed their only school skills: lower-level cognitive skills, memorization, and regurgitation of information.

This is great if you intend on going to school forever, but in the real world school skills are not relevant. Unless, as Seth Godin writes in his book, *Linchpin* (2010), "Your career involves homework assignments, looking through textbooks for answers that are already known to your supervisors, comply with instructions and then, in high-pressure settings, regurgitating those facts with limited processing on your part" (p. 47).

The bottom line is that schools must change drastically to reverse the growing disconnect between school life and real life. We need to prepare our students for their future, not our past. To do this our students will need to leave school with a different set of skills than they typically do today. We believe that the essential skills fall into six main categories (in addition to the traditional three Rs that continue to be important skills in the modern world). We call these six new skill categories the 21st-century fluencies.

We use the term *fluency* for a reason. It demonstrates a level of proficiency far beyond literacy. For example, you may be literate in a second language, but you still have to make a conscious effort to think about what you are hearing or reading to decode its meaning. However, when you are fluent in a second language, you have attained a certain comfort level so that its use is subconscious and automatic. Having a literacy-level use of skills is not enough. They need to be developed to a level of fluency, where they become internalized and are used subconsciously.

Solution Fluency

The first of these new essential 21st-century skills is solution fluency. This is about whole-brain ★ thinking—creativity and problem-solving skills applied in real time. Solution fluency is at the core of "just-in-time learning," which is essential to function successfully in the culture of the 21st century.

Information Fluency

The second new essential 21st-century skill is information fluency, which is comprised of two parts. Being able to access raw information from the most appropriate high-tech and low-tech sources is the first part. This may be from a textbook, but may just as easily be a cell phone, wiki, social network, other digital, or nontraditional source. Information sources are no longer exclusively text-based; they now include various mediums, including text, but also images, sound, and video.

Secondly, a person can't be considered to have information literacy, let alone information fluency, if all they can do is get information without the ability to critically evaluate the data they find. In the 24/7 InfoWhelm world, finding information is the easy part; what is really needed is the ability to find significant information. There is a need to be able to determine bias in the information we retrieve, assessing the accuracy of the data by analyzing the methodology of how it was gathered and cross-referencing it to multiple sources that verify and support the specific information that is found.

Collaboration Fluency

In the new digital landscape, collaboration has taken on a whole new meaning. Collaboration fluency is a teamworking proficiency that has reached the subconscious ability to work cooperatively with virtual and real partners in an online environment to create original digital products.

As we've already mentioned, companies and individuals are already working together in mass collaboration projects on a global scale. Virtual interaction has become part of the modern-day workflow, and we all need to be able to work with global virtual partners in order to function in the culture of the 21st century.

Creativity Fluency

Creative fluency is the process by which artistic proficiency adds meaning through design, art, and storytelling. It's no longer enough to have a functional product. In today's marketplace it is innovative design combined with a quality functioning product that is in demand.

Creative fluency extends beyond visual creative skills to using the imagination to create stories, ★ and to create products which tell stories, a practice which is in demand in many facets of today's economy. Creative minds to develop creative solutions, and with creativity fluency, the artistic creation of those solutions will transcend mere functionality. This essential ability is in high demand and will become even more important as new technologies expand our ability to create unimaginable solutions.

Media Fluency

There are two components of media fluency. The first component is the ability to look analytically at any communication media to interpret the real message, determine how the chosen media is being used to shape thinking, and evaluate the efficacy of the message. The second component is the ability to create and publish original digital products, matching the media to the intended message by determining the most appropriate and effective media for that message.

Publishing is no longer the domain of a few companies and select developers. In our multimedia world anyone can communicate their message to the rest of the world through a wide range of media. For our students to communicate effectively in a multimedia world, they will have to transcend text communication and be able to communicate with sound, video, and imagery. They will utilize the principles of graphic design as effectively as they can with text.

The Digital Citizen

All the 21st-century fluencies are learned within the context of the digital citizen, using the guiding principles of leadership, ethics, accountability, fiscal responsibility, environmental awareness, global citizenship, and personal responsibility. The concept of "digital citizenship" has been the topic of several books, the most comprehensive of which is *Digital Communities, Digital Citizenship: Perspectives for Educators* by Dr. Jason Ohler (2010).

This is only a brief overview of the 21st-century fluencies; there is much more to say, and we discuss them in depth in our book, *Literacy Is Not Enough: 21st Century Fluencies for the Digital Age* (Jukes, McCain, & Crockett, 2010).

We want to point out that noticeably absent from this list is any kind of technology fluency. Many people think 21st-century fluencies are about technology, but they are not. This is because technology has become ubiquitous. It's everywhere, and the digital generation assimilates it as fast as manufacturers can produce it. Give any of them a new digital gadget and they will figure out how it works before you can finish reading the safety precautions in the manual.

Technology isn't the problem anymore, so the 21st-century fluencies are not about technology, but what to do with it. They are process skills and critical thinking skills that are indicative of the kind of skills that everyone will need in the digital age.

Summarizing the Main Points

- We don't focus on critical thinking and problem-solving skills in school.

- We have lost sight of the need for our students to become independent thinkers and doers.

- We need to prepare our students for their future, not our past.

- Technology has become ubiquitous. The 21st-century fluencies are not about technology, but what to do with it.

Some Questions to Consider

- Where are you going to work and live?

- What sort of future do you have to look forward to?

- How many of you know what you are going to do once you leave school?

- How will you deal with all the changes that are coming your way?

- Do you have the necessary math, science, language arts, and technical skills that are needed for even entry-level employment?

- If not, where and how are you going to get them?

Chapter 13
New Roles for Educators

> In order to transform schools successfully, educators need to navigate the difficult space between letting go of old patterns and grabbing on to new ones.
>
> **Terrence E. Deal**

With a world experiencing the kind of change we have outlined in this book, coupled with the dramatic changes that we see occurring in the near future, clearly there will be new demands on schools to prepare students for the dynamically new environment they will face upon graduation.

In the previous chapter, we described the major shift in emphasis on the kinds of skills students will need for success in the future. A shift of this magnitude will force teachers to examine their role in the learning endeavor. It is clear that the new skills will necessitate a shift in the roles teachers take in facilitating learning for their students, but what will these new roles be, and how can we project what they will be in these times of exponential change? The key is to look for those roles that transcend the specifics of how we do our daily tasks because how we do our daily tasks will surely change. We must identify the broad new roles that will endure as the world continues to change dramatically. As we consider what these new roles will be, we also must be careful not to throw the baby out with the bathwater. The essence of what we must do in the future is the very same as it always has been for educators—to help their students learn the relevant skills, knowledge, attitudes, attributes, and behaviors that they will need to be good and productive citizens, parents, and workers in the nation.

Let's consider some of the new functions and responsibilities for teachers in light of what we have discussed thus far in this book.

Educators as People With a Dual Focus

Over the past 30 years, educators have become increasingly single-minded. As we have already mentioned, out of necessity, teachers have become fixated on the present. Driven by educational legislation, teachers and administrators use test data from the previous year to inform decisions one year at a time. There is a fixation on looking at test results and using them to determine how we can use them to develop strategies that will get our students ready for the test at the end of the school year. Driven by the mandates of high-stakes testing and accountability for all, we tend to focus on the next day, the next topic, the next test, and the next term. Year after year we find ourselves in the same vicious loop.

A casualty of this short-term focus is the consideration of long-term goals in the preparation, instruction, and evaluation we do. These are the broader targets we have for our students, the major goals we have for preparing them to be good people, effective citizens, and productive workers. They include equipping them with the 21st-century fluencies we discussed in the previous chapter. These long-term goals are too important to ignore if we want to adequately prepare our students for the life that awaits them upon graduation. However, these long-term targets seem to get overwhelmed by the urgent daily demands of covering our curriculum and getting students ready to perform on tests.

All teachers agree that the long-term goals should be addressed. The question is, how do we accomplish both the short-term and the long-term goals at the same time? To do both of these things, teachers will need to learn to have a dual focus, seeing the world on a split screen with daily life and all its demands on one side and, by living life like a quarterback, seeing the future with all its possibilities and probabilities on the other. On one side of the screen, teachers must be pragmatic, dealing with the realities of teaching in the school system. On the other side of the screen, teachers must be futurists, anticipating what will be coming next. We are not referring to gazing into a crystal ball. Rather, what we are suggesting is a reasoned extrapolation of current trends to project what will happen as those trends unfold in the future. To be effective in times of exponential change, teachers must begin to anticipate the future by doing their own trend analysis to make their teaching useful for more than just today. Being able to do this is crucial to keeping instruction future-relevant. In addition, as teachers begin to practice this, they are doing more than just staying on top of change. They are also providing students with a good model for how to deal with change.

Educators as Guides

The traditional approach to education that has been entrenched in the school system for more than a hundred years has a content focus. Students are viewed as vessels to be filled up with knowledge of facts, dates, names, places, events, and procedures. This knowledge is passed from the knowledge expert in the classroom—the teacher—through lectures, reading of textbooks, handouts, and library books and, today, reading online information sources. The idea is that once this information is committed to memory, students will become educated in how the world works and how it got to where it is today. Thus, in this approach the main method for assessing the education level of a student has been measuring the student's ability to recall their knowledge of facts, dates, names, places, events, and procedures on written tests.

The problem is that this model for instruction does not hold up in the age of exponential change and InfoWhelm. Technical scientific information is changing at an astounding rate, rendering much of what we know out of date very quickly. While historical events and writing does not change, the studies on history, literature, art, music, and poetry are cascading onto the scene at a terrific pace, continually changing our understanding of and opinions on their significance. The speed at which this new information enters our lives makes it more and more difficult for teachers to be the experts they once were. This world of ever-increasing change is forcing us to rethink the idea of the teacher at the front of the classroom telling students what they need to know. Technology is changing too rapidly and the amount of information in the world is increasing too quickly for any one person to have complete knowledge in any specific area. The idea that in today's world a teacher could be the primary source of information in a classroom is becoming increasingly absurd.

It's time to abandon the idea of teachers as vessel fillers and start to consider students as fires to be kindled. Teachers must become out-and-out arsonists, igniting a roaring blaze of passion for learning in their students and themselves that sustains itself not just to the next day or class, but for a lifetime. But how do we do this? We need to move away from being the sage on the stage and move toward becoming the guide on the side in the classroom. This is a monumental shift in the role of the teacher. If the teacher is not going to be the one who is always telling students about the world, then they must increasingly move to the side to direct the students into discovering things about the world.

We need to understand that educators have a new and different role to play as guides. Being a good educator is about more than good classroom management. It's about creating an engaging methodology that compels students to do much more than learn. It's about getting them to want to learn. Without them wanting to learn, there will be no meaningful long-term learning. This is about showing students how to follow the trails to learning for themselves, or to blaze their own trails. Educators must encourage students to go further and in different directions from the traditional beaten paths learners have always followed. To do this, we need to move away from being classroom controllers and managers and move toward being peer and team learning facilitators.

Educators as Process Instructors

Students forget content. Any teacher knows this. Ask a student a question that they answered correctly two weeks after they wrote a test and chances are they have already forgotten some, if not all, of the specific information they memorized in preparation for the test. Think back to the classes you took when you were in high school. How much specific detail do you remember? Much has been forgotten. What stays with us are the process skills. These skills include the traditional literacy skills of how to read, how to write, and how to do numerical calculations. They also include the 21st-century fluency skills of how to solve problems, how to search for information, and how to evaluate information when it is found, how to create effective multimedia communications, and how to collaborate with virtual coworkers. Process skills are much more powerful than simply remembering specific detail because process skills can be applied over and over again in many different circumstances with very different specific details. Process skills are also much more useful for students to acquire because they are remembered long after specific information is forgotten.

But teaching process skills is easier said then done. Teachers face a daunting task each and every day with the daily demands of instructing young children or adolescents, dealing with their parents, covering the curriculum that must be taught, responding to the demands of administrators, preparing engaging lessons, creating and marking tests, and preparing students for larger standardized evaluations. And with the increasing pressure to increase student test performance that we have experienced over the last 10 to 15 years, the natural response of teachers has been to ignore focusing on process skills and focus instead on short-term information recall in their instruction. And while educators have long aspired to the teaching of the process skills of higher-order thinking (like analysis, synthesis, and evaluation that are critical to effective problem solving), teaching and assessing lower-level skills like the memorization of specific curriculum content, basic spelling, grammar, and basic arithmetic skills takes up so much of the time that we don't often get to those higher-level skills that we think are so important. It can be very frustrating.

So what is to be done? Teachers want to shift the focus of instruction to higher-level process skills, but the demands of teaching the lower-level skills eats up so much of our time and effort it is very difficult to make room to make this shift happen. One way out of this dilemma is for teachers to let go of something they are doing now in order to have the time to focus on something new. The obvious choice is to let go of some of the teaching and assessing of lower-level skills. Digital technologies can offer teachers some real hope in this area. New technologies are increasingly being given the capacity to assist in the teaching of lower-level thinking tasks of the curriculum. Using these new tools, educators will be able to explore instruction where more emphasis is placed on the teaching of higher-level process skills. Teachers must be willing to embrace partnerships with nonhuman electronic assistants. But this represents a quantum leap for many educators. There will be great feelings of discomfort and fear of losing control because traditionally, teachers have been in charge of all of the instruction that takes place in the classroom.

> *The obvious choice is to let go of some of the teaching and assessing of lower-level skills. Digital technologies can offer teachers some real hope in this area.*

These feelings of disorientation are predictable. The rest of the world has been dealing with the phenomenon of technologically induced change for some time. It is important that teachers realize that instability is a normal consequence of the development of technological power. No matter where it is has been applied, powerful new electronic technology has fundamentally destabilized the status quo.

New tools and techniques quickly render traditional methods obsolete. Since the school system has been stable for such a long time, the instability that will result from the use of new electronic tools for instruction will be considerable. Teachers, especially those who have been teaching for a long time, will find the next few years very challenging. However, we must persist because one of the great benefits of the appropriate use of new technological tools is more time for teachers to focus on the teaching of higher-level skills. Never has that old saw about giving someone a fish versus teaching them to fish been more appropriate than it is today.

Educators as Crafters of Problems

The traditional approach to instruction focuses on content delivery. And while a teacher can cover a lot of material, the amount of learning by the students is usually less than what is desired. The problem is that engagement is frequently a casualty when the focus is on content because the material is often given without context. One of the criticisms often leveled at teachers who use this content-driven approach is that they give the answers to students before they have any questions. A great challenge teachers face is how to deliver the content in a course curriculum while creating the engagement in the learning activities and providing a context for the content that is necessary for long-term learning to occur.

We have suggested that teachers must embrace a new role as a guide in the learning process. But if teachers are going to move to the side in their instruction, then they must find an alternative to the traditional approach of telling students about the content in the courses they have to teach. One effective alternative is to shift teaching away from telling students things to presenting them with problems. Problems give students a reason for learning new information. They also create questions in the students' minds, which naturally engages them in the learning activity. These questions also foster student ownership of the learning. For these reasons, it is important that teachers embrace the role as the crafter of problems.

The skill in constructing problems involves considering a number of factors. Teachers must take the material in the course curriculum guide and craft problems that are appropriate for the intellectual and social development of their students while leading them into all the specific detail of the information that must be covered. To ensure that the task produces the engagement and relevance necessary for effective learning, the problem should have a link to the world outside school. Developing the skill of crafting these kinds of learning activities needs to be a priority for teachers. *Teaching for Tomorrow*, the next book in the 21st Century Fluency series, outlines more fully an instructional approach based on crafting and presenting problems to students.

Educators as Facilitators of 21st-Century Fluencies

Acquiring proficiency in the traditional literacies of the three Rs is not enough to prepare students for the technologically rich, multimedia, InfoWhelm world of the 21st century. It's a world that is not only changing daily—it is changing exponentially. To be ready for success in the environment they will encounter in the future, students must master both the traditional basic skills plus the new 21st-century fluencies we have already discussed. The demands of the new digital world make teaching these fluencies to our students an instructional imperative.

The 21st-century fluencies we have presented represent a significant shift in the target teachers must aim for in their instruction. Teaching these fluencies by adopting the new roles we have presented thus far will require teachers to change their approach to teaching and, in many cases, change significantly. A person can't continue to do things the same way they always have and expect to get different results. No, different results require different methods. Therefore, teachers must embrace these new and different roles in the learning endeavor because they will produce different results. To begin moving away from traditional ideas for instruction, teachers must develop a dual focus—they must maintain a focus on both the daily demands of teaching young people as well as on the direction the world is heading in the longer term so they can adjust their instruction appropriately. Teachers must also shift away from being front and center in the classroom to being a guide and coach from the sidelines so students can do more of the learning for themselves. Teachers must shift their focus away from teaching for content recall to teaching the processes to empower students to become independent thinkers. Teachers must move away from seeing teaching as talking to an approach that presents students with problems to solve so that students will be able to accomplish tasks on their own. Teachers must also embrace the teaching of the 21st-century fluencies to keep their instruction relevant and to adequately prepare their students for the realities of the modern world.

When all these new roles are taken together, it becomes clear that the task of teaching 21st-century fluencies involves much more facilitation than it involves traditional direct instruction. Teachers must gain sufficient expertise in the fluencies to be able to guide students in their learning, but teachers must resist the temptation to pass on their expertise through traditional teaching. Instead, they must give students tasks that challenge them to solve problems, sort through contradictory and/or incomplete information, interpret messages in multimedia formats, create imaginative ways to communicate, and work with virtual coworkers who may not even be awake when work is being done. And this must be done with a strategy of progressive withdrawal of the teacher from assisting students so they can do these tasks independently.

Educators as Users of Technology

In the new digital landscape, the use of digital tools isn't optional. Technology is a daily reality in the personal and working lives of people outside the school system. School must reflect that reality. It is imperative that teachers embrace the role of using technology themselves and facilitating the use of digital tools with their students. Instead of banning digital devices, we should be encouraging students to use them. This is not just about being "progressive." This is because we live in a digital network culture where the use of digital tools is the new reality of both business and personal life. A young person simply cannot leave school without relevant technology skills and succeed in modern life. Teachers must become advocates for getting current technology into their classrooms so that all students can benefit from its use. Schools are supposed to be the great equalizers in democratic society. This means that we should provide disadvantaged students with the same opportunities to use technology as students from more affluent families.

Educators as Holistic Evaluators

Assessment is about getting a picture of a student's learning. The traditional tools for getting this picture have been written reports and essays and written tests. While these tools do measure a certain part of learning, the question is, do they provide a complete picture of student learning? Reports, essays, and paper-based tests predominantly reflect memory and the regurgitation of content, primarily from textbooks. This content-based approach promotes a "teach, test, and turf" model, where we fill kids up with content so they can recall it upon request—and then they forget it. This must end.

Let's consider what constitutes the learning a student must do in school to be able to function in the modern world upon graduation. Understanding the increasingly disposable nature of information, memorization of specific content will decrease in importance in the future. Instead, students must learn to follow and apply processes in order to accomplish tasks—the writing process, the research process, and the problem-solving process, just to name three. Determining the relative importance of various pieces of information that may be contradictory and/or incomplete, then making personal evaluations of that information to develop informed opinions, is a critical component of student learning. Articulating informed opinions through writing, presentations, debates, and various multimedia communications is fundamental to a student's learning. Using imagination to produce creative expressions of ideas and feelings through story, poetry, music, visual art, and performing art is increasingly important in modern life. Another essential component of learning involves combining technical skill and creativity to cook a meal, build a desk, customize a car, perform an experiment, and so on. Learning also encompasses social skill development and the consideration of others. When all of these components are taken together, we get a complete picture of student learning.

The problem we have in the evaluation of learning is that traditional assessment tools like reports, essays, quizzes, and tests only capture a small part of the picture we outlined in the previous paragraph. It is imperative that we embrace other forms of evaluation or develop new ones if we hope to do an adequate job of assessing the learning students do in school. One reason for the urgency to consider an expanded set of assessment tools is that evaluation drives instruction. If teachers realize that no matter what other learning takes place in their classroom, all they and their students will get credit for is performance on written tests, then that is exactly what teachers will focus on. The tragedy of this is that many of those components that students, parents, and prospective employers are looking for are diminished or discarded entirely in the push for test scores.

Therefore, it is vital that teachers become holistic evaluators. All facets of learning must be esteemed in the assessment we do of student learning. Portfolios of student work, live performances, and other demonstrations of creativity and competency must be considered when attempting to get a complete picture of the progress of a student. Teachers must also embrace a shift away from viewing assessment as just measuring learning after a task has been completed. Evaluation in the 21st century has to help students get better at what they do. Assessment must shift to match the teacher's new role as a guide and so ongoing assessment with a goal of providing feedback so students can improve their

This content-based approach promotes a "teach, test, and turf" model, where we fill kids up with content so they can recall it upon request—and then they forget it. This must end.

performance needs to become much more a part of what teachers do. Students need timely, targeted, nonjudgmental feedback on their performance. They need opportunities to make mistakes as they learn and not be penalized for them. And they need authentic audiences in a variety of settings and contexts in which to demonstrate what they can do. But most of all, they need the encouragement to try to do things in all kinds of performance areas with all kinds of tools, technologies, and techniques to create all kinds of products that reflect their understanding of concepts. For this to happen, we need to rethink assessment and evaluation and go beyond the traditional quantitative summative assessment of learning that doesn't really help the students get better.

Educators as Modelers

It's a widespread observation that students not only do what we say, they also model what we do. They also subconsciously model our thought processes and pick up on what we value. This is an important point, often missed by educators. For example, teachers often demonstrate that they value the product students hand in rather than the thought process required to create it. This can be seen both in how we teach and how we evaluate student learning.

Ted McCain can remember a clear example of how he valued product over process from his own teaching. The situation was the teaching of a proof in a mathematics class. When he reached the end of the proof, it didn't work out. He remembers feeling upset, embarrassed, and defeated. As a result, he went away and worked on that proof at home until he could do it forward and backward. Next math class, when he completed the proof on the board, his students only saw the end result of the learning process he had gone through. They never got to see the struggle, the thinking, and the mess involved in his solving the problem at home. It's little wonder that his students then felt upset and defeated. It wasn't until years later that he realized he had done his students a great disservice. He had presented them with a finished product that was unattainable to them because he didn't model the learning process they needed to go through to get there.

In terms of evaluation, many teachers clearly tell their students that product is far more important than process. Here's one example of how they do it. We know that there are five distinct steps in the writing process: planning, drafting, revising, proofing, and publishing. Most teachers know that the key to good writing is to have their students progress through each of the steps in the process. However, when it comes to assessing student learning, they focus completely on the end product, giving little, if any, marks for successfully following through the five steps in the process. The students quickly learn that regardless of what the teacher says, the only thing that counts is the final product. No wonder we have trouble getting students to revise their writing once it's done.

> It's a widespread observation that students not only do what we say, they also model what we do.

When educators place too much emphasis on the product to be created, it really doesn't help students learn because they don't see the realities of how real learning takes place. The thinking skills in the processes behind the products are what empower the students to do the creating. Many teachers don't like showing the processes involved in wrestling with new concepts and skills because real learning and thinking is a messy business. But those messy thinking skills absolutely need to be our focus. Ted has since changed his teaching approach, and he now puts much more emphasis on the thinking involved in problem solving. He models everything from asking questions to analyzing possible solutions to working them through, even if they don't work out. He has realized that getting students to apply a structured thought process is the key to successfully teaching his students to think mathematically.

Almost as important as what we do is what we do *not* do. Amazingly, our students also model what we do not do. If you stop and think about it for a moment, you will see there are three sets of curriculum in every classroom. The first is the explicit curriculum as outlined by the state or province. The second is the implicit curriculum we learn from the teacher's values. The third is what we will call the null curriculum—that which we learn from what teachers don't do.

Consider the null curriculum as it might apply to the many students today who are told technology is important, but at the same time work with teachers who do not, or will not, use it. Even today in a world profoundly affected by the explosion of technology in our lives, many educators take the attitude that technology might be a great tool, but it's not their job to learn it, to use it, or to teach it. They see no connection between the subject matter they teach and new technologies. By refusing to see or even consider the connections, trends, and tremendous change engulfing the world, teachers are sending students the unspoken message that technology really is not very important. Thus, it is critical that educators recognize the impact of what we model to our students. We need to focus on the positive power our actions can have in fostering the attitudes and behaviors students need for success.

Educators as Lifelong Learners

As the prospect of being an all-knowing teacher fades into the past, educators are beginning to understand that they must make the transition from teaching their students to learning with their students and even to learning from their students. Transforming our professional practices to include continual learning is a powerful teaching strategy that enables educators to maintain relevance by becoming excellent role models, learning guides, process instructors, and futurists. Being open to and embracing all the skills necessary for taking on new instructional roles is critical as we move into the new millennium.

If the education system is to survive and rise to the challenges facing it in the 21st century, the system must take on the qualities of a learning organization and the teachers must take on the qualities of new millennium learners. A learning organization, as defined by Peter Senge, is a community of autonomous people who skillfully, consciously, and responsibly cooperate with others to build the enormous human potential in their dynamic roles as producers, consumers, and community members. A learning organization seeks to create its own future. It assumes that learning is an ongoing and creative process. It develops, adapts, and transforms itself in response to the needs and aspirations of people it connects with.

As educators in the new millennium, we must see ourselves as members of a learning organization where our own learning makes the organization stronger and keeps it relevant. One can't be static in such an organization. For many teachers, this will mean realizing there is a big difference between teaching for 15 years and teaching one year 15 times. We must all recognize that we are in a learning business. As such, we must realize that we will be teaching, but we will also be simultaneously learning with and from our students.

A Need for a Massive Shift in the Training and Retraining of Teachers

To teach in the future, educators will need more than just a few professional days devoted to technology use or problem-based learning. They will need to make a fundamental shift in their paradigm for teaching and learning. We must start by recognizing that the current educational system has been set up to prepare students perfectly for a world that no longer exists. We must embrace the fact that massive, ongoing retraining for educators is essential if schools are to be made relevant to the needs of all of our students and if we are to properly prepare them for the world that awaits them once they graduate.

However, to bring about this substantial change in how teachers view their roles in the classroom, we must address two major impediments to teacher retraining. The first is the fact that traditional school culture is not used to change. The current school system is probably one of the most stable institutions existing in the world today. Our school year was initially set in the 1800s to meet the demands of an agricultural society that required children to help harvest the crops. The school system has had very little real competition for our students. The basic organizational structure was set for the Industrial Age of the assembly line. The majority of our teachers employ instructional methods that have been used for hundreds of years.

While the rest of the world has undergone radical and repeated restructuring over the last 15 to 20 years, schools have remained remarkably unaffected by these sweeping changes. All of these factors have led to a strong, subconscious resistance to change. As a result, many teachers believe that change happens somewhere else to someone else—that somehow education is immune to the disruptive forces happening outside of education.

The second impediment to teacher retraining is the very nature of the job of teaching itself. Despite the perception of much of the public and the media, teaching is a difficult and challenging job that is full of stress. Teachers are asked to do a great number of things beyond teaching, and their plates are always full. Making the kinds of changes we are suggesting here will never happen using the current model of teachers taking four or five professional development days a year to tackle the wide range of organizational, instructional, and student behavior problems associated with running a school.

Therefore, schools of the future will have to embrace the kind of retraining models that have proven effective in the business world. Many companies have realized that to be truly effective in reeducating their work force, they have to remove their workers from their regular work for extended period of time so they can focus on the task of learning. Many companies have built training centers and have a significant portion of their workers attending retraining classes on an ongoing basis.

Schools will have to do the same. Retraining will require regular classes for teachers for which they are released from their regular teaching duties. If we want to see the kinds of changes necessary to bring schools in line with the new reality, then we have no option but to radically reprioritize and restructure professional development for teachers.

Summarizing the Main Points

- New skills necessitate a shift in the roles teachers take in facilitating learning for their students.

- Teachers need to learn to have a dual focus, seeing the world on a split screen with daily life and all its demands on one side, and seeing the future with all its possibilities and probabilities on the other.

- Process skills are much more powerful than simply remembering specific detail.

- One of the great benefits of the appropriate use of new technological tools is more time for teachers to focus on the teaching of higher-level skills.

- The demands of the new digital world make teaching the 21st-century fluencies to our students an instructional imperative.

- Teachers must become advocates for getting current technology into their classrooms so that all students can benefit from its use.

- We must rethink assessment and evaluation and go beyond the traditional quantitative summative assessment of learning.

- We need to focus on the positive power our actions can have in fostering the attitudes and behaviors students need for success.

- If we want to see the kinds of changes necessary to bring schools in line with the new reality, then we have no option but to radically reprioritize and restructure professional development for teachers.

Some Questions to Consider

- Based on what you have just read, brainstorm on the topic of what it will mean to be educated in the 21st century.

- Based on what you have read, what do you understand now that you didn't understand before, and why is it important?

- Based on what you have just read, what are three things you have learned today, and how will you use them?

- What advice would you give the administration, school board members, or politicians to ensure that the issues of change, as outlined in this book, are addressed appropriately in our schools?

- What strategies do you have for keeping yourself up-to-date on developments in your field of expertise? What magazines, newsletters, online newsgroups, specialty web sites, and other sources exist to help you with this task? Make a list of these sources and then develop a plan for butterfly hunting every day. What unexamined assumptions about present schooling do we need to consider?

- What would an ideal future-oriented school look like?

Chapter 14
A Need for Vision

> My interest is in the future, because I'm going to spend the rest of my life there.
>
> **Charles F. Kettering**

These are absolutely amazing, astounding, challenging times that were perfectly summarized more than 100 years ago by the great British-American philosopher Alfred North Whitehead when he said this:

> *It is the business of the future to be dangerous. The major advances in civilization are processes that all but wreck the societies in which they occur.*

We have to keep in mind that the long term is no longer measured in centuries or decades, but increasingly in terms of years and sometimes months, weeks, days, or even hours. We live in a moment in history where change has become so fast that we begin to see the present only when it is already disappearing into the past. As a result, our biggest challenge is and will continue to be comprehending and accepting the scale of change—change that is happening so rapidly that the very nature of change is changing.

When changes are happening quickly, we tend to hang on to old ideas and assumptions about the world. When we do this, we run the risk of ending up crashing headlong into the future. This is perfectly summarized by the great philosopher Erik Hoffer, who once said:

> *In times of radical change the learners inherit the Earth; while the learned find themselves perfectly equipped for a world that no longer exists.*

Our greatest fear is that despite our very best intentions to do what's right for our students, because of our mindsets we might just as easily be preparing them for a world that no longer exists.

This all starts with understanding the origin and basis of our current paradigms because this helps open the windows to the future more fully and allows us to make sense of the changes that are at work in the world today. It is only in getting beyond our own paradigm paralysis and embracing new ways of thinking that we can begin to harness the astonishing power of the forces that have been unleashed upon us through the proliferation of new technologies.

Unless we can step back from all that is happening and learn to deal with change and the changing nature of change, simply peering through the windows into the future will leave us as little more than passive observers as the world passes us by.

Throughout this book, we have stressed that when looking through windows to the future, it is essential to move beyond seeing to perceiving. This requires the ability to anticipate where things are going and to expect the unexpected. Perceiving the future through what is happening in the present requires vision.

The great American writer and thinker, Helen Keller, was blind, deaf, and mute early in her life, but she overcame these profound handicaps to become one of America's most eloquent spokespersons for the possibilities of life. Despite her many handicaps, she became a university professor, the author of more than 30 books, and a great visionary.

Helen Keller was approached by one of her students and asked how she felt about being blind. She responded by simply remarking that the only thing worse than not being able to see is being able to see and having no vision. Her statement applies equally as well today when we consider how to deal with the many possibilities of global exponential change. More than anything else, it requires people with vision.

Living on the Future Edge is intended to provide interpretation, understanding, context, and vision to the multitude of changes that are happening, as well as to the implications these changes have for our future. We are asking you to stand back and take the longer view to begin to understand some of the possibilities for our children, our schools, our communities, our businesses, and society at large.

That's why we wrote this book. We looked through several different windows on the future. We introduced you to the concept of paradigms and asked you to consider your own paradigms and the effects these mindsets have had on how you view and use technology. We examined the technology of change, discussed the key developments in technological development, and described the effects that accelerated change has on the compression of development. We described how one must live life like a quarterback as an effective strategy for dealing with accelerated change and then used that strategy to consider six global exponential trends that are central to the future of education: Moore's Law, photonics, the Internet, nanotechnology, biotechnology, and InfoWhelm. We made a call to arms and declared that it was time for education to catch up to this new digital landscape. We considered how these global exponential trends will affect education and identified the new skills needed to live, work, and learn in a rapidly changing world. We outline new roles for educators and for learners as we shifted from a focus on teaching to a focus on learning. Then, we provided a series of scenarios for teaching and learning in the future.

So where do you start? We passionately believe that change does not start with us or our issues and our comfort zones. Change starts with our children, our hopes, our dreams, and our prayers for their future. Our children may only be 25 percent of the population but they are 100 percent of the future of our nations.

We must begin by facing the facts. We live in a new and very different world—one that is constantly re-creating and redefining itself. Changing our schools is essential if our children are to be properly prepared for the world that continues to change exponentially. Economic, technological, informational, demographic, and political forces have and continue to transform the way people live and work. Our schools, like our businesses, our communities, and our families, must constantly adapt to changing conditions to thrive.

That's why we need to develop new schools that will prepare students for their future—for the life ahead of them after they leave school—for the rest of their lives. And yes, we know this is hard. As educators, we must understand that our job is not just to serve what is or has been, but to shape what can, what might, and what must be.

Education is a major issue in the post-industrial society in which we live. This is fundamentally an issue of national security because schools are our farms of the future. Imagine what would have happened in the Industrial Age if we had run out of iron ore. Imagine what will happen in the new Information Age if we run out of primary resource, which is thinking minds. Schools produce our most valuable crop—the most essential raw material for our Information Age economy.

How do we leverage these powerful new technologies to bring about the meaningful and lasting change in schools that will ensure our continued economic success in the modern, changing world? How can we change the curriculum to reflect the growing power of new devices and the new mindsets they create? How do we retool what's already in place?

Education can't be a "gee whiz, we really should get around to changing things someday" sort of enterprise. It needs to be a fundamental priority for every individual, group, business, and institution in our society. To do this—to really change how students are educated—we need a different mindset that will allow us to discard many of the longstanding aspects of our cultural and institutional paradigms. We need to create the new schools that will teach the skills that will be necessary to function in this constantly changing world. We must do what is necessary to prepare students for their tomorrows rather than our yesterdays. We can no longer feel content with serving what exists—what has existed for decades. Rather, we must shape what can, what might, and what absolutely must be.

We must also face the fact that the world outside education has embraced the changes much more quickly than our educational institutions have. As a consequence, there is a growing gap between the skills, knowledge, attitudes, attributes, and behaviors that most students leave our schools with now, and what they need if they are going to survive, let alone thrive, in the culture of the 21st century.

> *As educators, we must understand that our job is not just to serve what is or has been, but to shape what can, what might, and what must be.*

What do we do about this gap? We must first recognize that throwing more technology at the problem won't really solve things. The real issue is the paradigm paralysis of teachers, administrators, parents, and politicians who have a rearview mirror mindset when it comes to what schools should be. In the end, the issue is not just a hardware issue. Increasingly, it's a headware issue. It's about critical thinking, problem solving, and the 21st-century fluencies. Educators must learn to get comfortable with these fluencies and use them to shape the vision of tomorrow.

Living on the Future Edge is a challenge to all of us, especially those in education, to become actively involved in this process of change. Many people still believe that education can and will continue on its present path and that change is something that happens to someone else. Business management guru James Crupi's observation summarizes it beautifully. He says that in times of radical change, there are three kinds of people in the world—those who make change happen, those who watch change happen, and those who don't know what hit them.

We believe that in order to become people who make change happen, those in the school system need to get beyond the *yabbuts*:

- yeah but, we don't have the staff development time to help teachers learn new curriculum or to change long-standing pedagogical practices
- yeah but, we don't have the financial resources to wire every classroom
- yeah but, we don't yet have the resources to put all of the tools in the hands of every child
- yeah but, we have no control over the curriculum because it's dictated by the state, by college entrance requirements, or by the school board
- yeah but, I'm only a few years from retirement
- yeah but, yeah but, yeah but . . .

Do your colleagues get that change is accelerating? Does your community understand? Do your school boards, administrators, and parents have a sense of urgency about making changes to the way we prepare kids for the world after graduation?

In a conversation recently, a longtime friend and colleague, Jason Ohler, asked our group, "How many of us will admit to having a small bad habit? You know what we're talking about. Maybe you smoke, eat a bit too much chocolate, bite your nails, watch too much TV, or maybe you like to shop a little too much."

All of us sheepishly raised our hands as Jason asked another question, "How easy is it to break a small habit?" The answer is that even making small changes is really, really hard. Sometimes it seems impossible.

When we are challenged to rethink education, we are not being asked just to change a few behaviors or habits like how we spend our money, what we put into our bodies, or how we spend our time. What we are being asked here is to reconsider some of the most fundamental, traditional, and embedded parts of our life experiences and our habits of mind. That is the big and very real challenge that educational administrators and educators face at this moment. We understand that change is hard, that change is messy, that change is uncomfortable! Given this, it's very easy to throw up our hands and walk away with a complete sense of being overwhelmed, helpless, and hopelessness. How can we overcome these feelings? Change is hard, and sometimes the challenge of change seems absolutely overwhelming, but as the great anthropologist Margaret Mead once said:

> *Never doubt that a small group of thoughtful committed people can change the world—indeed it is the only thing that ever has. . . .*

The bottom line is this: Change doesn't start with a president or prime minister, it doesn't start with a governor or premier, and it doesn't start with your superintendent or your principal. Change starts with you and me. Change starts here, and it starts now. We can't wait until the last minute for everyone else to change first.

Turning a Blue Whale

Consider the blue whale for a moment. It is the largest mammal and, at 190 decibels, the loudest mammal on Earth. It is the length of three Greyhound buses placed end to end. It weighs more than a fully loaded Boeing 737 jet. Its heart is nearly the size of a Volkswagen Beetle. And do you know how big its tongue is? The blue whale's tongue is 8 feet long and weighs 6,000 lbs. During its first year of life, a baby blue whale gains an estimated 15 lbs. (6 kg) an hour. To give you an idea of the massive scale of a blue whale, to turn 180 degrees takes 3 to 5 minutes.

Now, there are a lot of people who draw a strong parallel between blue whales and our schools. Both of them seem to take forever to turn around. From this perspective it seems hopeless, doesn't it?

It's time to shift our mindset. Let's compare a blue whale to a gigantic school of sardines that has the same mass as the whale. There is a fundamental difference between the way a blue whale turns around and the way a school of sardines turns around.

Unlike the whale, a school of sardines can turn almost instantly. How do they do it? Is it ESP? Twitter? Cell phones? It is none of the above. If you take a closer look at a school of sardines, what you notice is that although the fish appear to be swimming together, in reality at any one time there is a small number of fish that are beginning to swim in a different direction.

As they head off on this new course, they cause conflict, friction, and collisions with the other fish. When a critical mass of sardines is reached (not a huge number like 50 percent or 80 percent of the school, but only 15 to 20 percent, who are truly committed to the new direction), the rest of the school changes direction and goes with them—almost instantaneously!

If you stop for a moment and consider some of the major recent changes in the world, you'll see that huge swings in direction can happen very quickly. Isn't that exactly what happened in North America regarding our attitudes toward smoking or drinking and driving being health risks? Isn't this exactly what happened to our intolerance with bank fraud or politicians who lie? Isn't that exactly what happened in East Germany and the Soviet Union when the communist governments lost their grip?

Each of these changes seemed to occur overnight, although they were years in the making, and took a only small group of truly committed individuals to set the change in motion and make it happen.

It's no different when we consider the necessary changes to our schools. Are you willing to become a Committed Sardine (www.committedsardine.com)? Are you willing to swim against the flow, against conventional wisdom, against our long-standing and traditional practices, and begin to move our schools, our students, and our communities from where they are to where they need to be?

It's a complete myth that change takes time. It's making the decision to change that really takes time. So where and how do we begin? By understanding that the longest journey starts with a single step—that the greatest movement starts with a single individual. This means more than using rhetoric, because rhetoric alone can't reform schools. No, we need action behind our words if we want real change in our schools. That will mean we have to stop doing what we are doing now and start doing new things. So it's up to us to take up the challenge and look through the windows on the future to see our part in this great opportunity to create new schools for the new millennium.

Summarizing the Main Points

- We live in absolutely amazing, astounding, and challenging times of dramatic global, exponential trends that require us to develop a fundamentally new vision for living, working, and learning in the culture of the 21st century.

- The only way to deal with rapid change is to view the present as the past of the future, and to understand that we must view change as a continuum that moves from the past to the future.

- Economic, technological, informational, demographic, and political forces have transformed and continue to transform the way people live and work. These changes and the rate of change will continue to accelerate. So our schools, like businesses, communities, and families, must constantly adapt to changing conditions to thrive.

- Real change does not start by waiting for external forces to respond. It starts with you and me, and it starts here and now.

- Our job is not just to accept what is. It's to shape what can, what might, and what must be.

- It's not change that takes time. It's making the decision to change that really takes the time.

Some Questions to Consider

- Why is it that many educators feel so overwhelmed by change and yet there appears to be little movement?

- Why is there so much change, yet a continued call for change seems to be a constant theme?

- What will you need to know to be able to function in coming ages as a citizen, a parent, and an educator?

- What are you doing to anticipate the future and to identify the challenges you may be facing in a world of rapid change?

- Based on the book you have just read, brainstorm on the topic of what it will mean to be educated in the 21st century.

- Based on your reading of the book, what are three things you have learned today, and how will you use them?

- What advice would you give the administration, school board members, or politicians to ensure that the issues of change as outlined in this book are addressed appropriately in our schools?

- What strategies do you have for keeping yourself up-to-date on developments in your field of expertise? What sources exist to help you with this task? Make a list of these informational sources and then develop a plan to access them every day.

Bibliography

Alpert, J., & Hajaj, N. (2008, July). *We knew the web was big....* GoogleBlog, Inc.: http://googleblog.blogspot.com/2008/07/we-knew-web-was-big.html

Barker, J. & Erickson, S. W. (2005). *Five regions of the future: Preparing your business for tomorrow's technology revolution.* New York: Penguin Press.

Barker, J. (1992). *Future edge.* New York: W. Morrow.

Barker, J. (1993). *Paradigms: The business of discovering the future.* New York: HarperBusiness.

Barry, D. (1996). *Dave Barry in cyberspace.* New York: Random House.

Brooks, D. (2008, May 8). *The New York Times.* http://www.nytimes.com/2008/05/02/opinion/02brooks.html?_r=2&oref=slogin&oref=login)

Buck Institute for Education. (2003). *Project based learning handbook.* Novato, CA: Author.

Cairncross, F. (1997). *The death of distance—How the communications revolution will change our lives.* Boston: Harvard Press.

Canton, J. (2006). *The extreme future—The top trends that will reshape the world for the next 5, 10, and 20 years.* New York: Penguin.

Christensen, C., Horn, M., & Johnson, C. (2008). *Disrupting class: How disruptive innovation will change the way the world learns.* New York: McGraw-Hill.

Collins, A., & Halverson, R. (2009). *Rethinking education in the age of technology—The digital revolution and schooling in America.* New York: Teachers College Press.

Crossman, W. (2004). VIVO—*The coming age of talking computers.* Oakland, CA: Regent Press.

Crupi, J. (2000). *Executive 2000.* American Way Magazine: http://www.crupi.com/amerway.html

Darling-Hammond, L. (1997). *The right to learn: A blueprint for creating schools that work.* San Francisco: Jossey-Bass.

Drake, P. (2009, October). *Google vs. facebook.* Drake Direct: http://drakedirect.blogspot.com/2009/10/draft-facebook-article.html

Dryden, G., & Vos, J. (2009). *Unlimited—The new learning revolution and the seven keys to unlock it.* Auckland, New Zealand: The Learning Web.

Florida, R. (2003). *The rise of the creative class—And how it's transforming work, leisure, community and everyday life.* New York: Basic Books.

Friedman, T. (2005). *The world is flat: A brief history of the twenty-first century.* New York: Farrar, Straus and Giroux.

Friedman, T. (2008). *Hot, flat, and crowded—Why we need a green revolution and how it can renew America.* New York: Farrar, Straus and Giroux.

Gantz, J., & Reinsel, D. (2009, May). *As the economy contracts, the digital universe expands.* Framingham, MA: IDC.

Gardner, H. (1983). *Frames of mind—Theories of multiple intelligences.* New York: Basic Books.

Garreau, J. (2005). *Radical evolution—The promise and peril of enhancing our minds, bodies-and what it means to be human.* New York: Random House.

Gates, B. (1994, November). *Information at your fingertips (2005).* Las Vegas, NV.: Comdex.

Gilder, G. (2000). *Telecosm: The world after bandwidth abundance.* New York: Free Press.

Gilder, G. (2005). *The silicon eye: How a silicon valley company aims to make all current c,mputers, cameras, and cell phones obsolete.* New York: Atlas Books.

Giles, J. (2005, December). *Internet encyclopedias go head to head.* Nature: 438, 900-901. http://www.nature.com/nature/journal/v438/n7070/full/438900a.html

Gilster, P. (1997). *Digital literacy.* New York: Wiley.

Godin, S. (2010). *Linchpin: Are you indispensable?* New York: Penguin.

James, J. (1996). *Thinking in future tense: Leadership skills for a new age.* New York: Simon & Schuster.

Jukes, I., McCain, T., & Crockett L. (2010). *Literacy is not enough—21st century fluencies for the digital age.* Kelowna, BC, Canada: 21st Century Fluency Project.

Kelly, F., McCain, T., & Jukes, I. (2008). *Teaching the digital generation—No more cookie cutter high schools.* Thousand Oaks, CA: Corwin.

Kurzweil, R. (2005). *The singularity is near—When humans transcend biology.* New York: Viking Press.

Lee, L. (2000). *Bad predictions—2000 years of the best minds making the worst forecasts.* Rochester, NY: Elsewhere Press.

Levy, F., & Murnane, R. J. (2005). *The new division of labor—How computers are creating the next job market.* Princeton, NJ: Princeton University Press.

Mace, M. (2010, February). *How many kindles have really been sold (and other interesting tidbits about ebooks).* Mobile Opportunity: http://mobileopportunity.blogspot.com/2010/02/how-many-kindles-have-really-been-sold.html

Makice, K. (2010, May) *Togetherville: A digital training ground for young geeks.* Wired Magazine: http://www.wired.com/geekdad/2010/05/togetherville-a-digital-training-ground-for-young-geeks/

Marzano, R. (2003). *What works in schools: Translating research into action.* ASCD: Alexandria, VA.

McCain, T. (2005). *Teaching for tomorrow: Teaching content and problem-solving skills.* Thousand Oaks, CA: Corwin.

McCain, T., & Jukes, I. (2000). *Windows on the future: Education in the age of technology.* Thousand Oaks, CA: Corwin.

Medina, J. (2008). *Brain rules.* Seattle, WA: Pear Press.

Moore, G. (1965, April). *Cramming more components onto integrated circuits.* Electronics Magazine: Vol.38, No. 8. New York: McGraw-Hill

Moravic, H. (1990). *Mind children: The future of robot and human intelligence.* Cambridge, MA: Harvard University Press.

Naisbitt, J. (2006). *Mind set!* New York: HarperCollins.

Ohler, J. (2010). *Digital communities, digital citizenship: Perspectives for educators.* Thousand Oaks, CA: Corwin.

Oppenheimer, T. (1997, July). The computer delusion. Washington, DC: The Atlantic Monthly

Palfrey, J., & Gasser, U. (2008). *Born digital—Understanding the first generation of digital natives*. New York: Basic Books.

Penn, M., & Zalesne, K. (2007). *Microtrends—The small forces behind tomorrow's big changes*. New York: Hachette.

Pink, D. (2006). *A whole new mind*. New York: The Berkley Publishing Group.

Poscente, V. (2008). *The age of speed: Learning to thrive in a more-faster-now world*. Austin, TX: Bard Press.

Prensky, M. (2006). *Don't bother me, mom—I'm learning*. St. Paul, MN: Paragon House.

Prensky, M. (2010). *Teaching digital natives: Partnering for real learning*. Thousand Oaks, CA: Corwin.

PriMetrica,Inc. (2006, December). *International carriers' traffic grows despite skype poularity*. TeleGeography Update: http://www.telegeography.com/cu/article.php?article_id=15656&email=html

Royal Pingdom. (2010, January). *Internet 2009 in numbers*. http://royal.pingdom.com/2010/01/22/internet-2009-in-numbers/

Rushkoff, D. (1999). *Playing the future: What can we learn from digital kids?* New York: Riverhead.

Senge, P. (1990). *The fifth discipline: The art and practice of the learning organization*. New York: Random House.

Shenk, D. (1997). *Data smog: Surviving the information glut*. San Francisco: HarperCollins.

Shirky, C. (2008). *Here comes everybody: The power of organizing with organizations*. New York: Penguin Press.

Smith, A. (1979). *Powers of the mind*. New York: Ballantine.

Sunstein, R. S. (2006). *Infotopia: How many minds produce knowledge?* New York: Oxford University Press.

Tapscott, D. (2009). *Grown up digital: How the net generation is changing your world*. New York: McGraw-Hill.

Tapscott, D., & Williams, A. (2006). *Wikinomics*. New York: The Penguin Group.

Taylor, F. (1911). *The principles of scientific management*. New York: Harper and Row.

Thornburg, D. (1992). *Edutrends 2010: Restructuring, technology, and the future of education*. San Carlos, CA: Starsong Publications.

Thornburg, D. (1996). *Campfires in cyberspace*. CUE: Santa Clara, CA.

Trump, J. L. (1959). *Images of the future*. Urbana, Ill., University of California: Commission on the Experimental Study of Utilization of the Staff in Secondary School.

Tweney, D. (2010, April). April 19, 1965: *How do you like it? Moore, moore, moore*. Wired Magazine: http://www.wired.com/thisdayintech/2010/04/0419moores-law-published/#ixzz0uQ2U72Fd

Twist, J. (2005, Aprl). *Law that has driven digital life*. BBC News: http://news.bbc.co.uk/2/hi/science/nature/4449711.stm

Wagner, T. (2008). *The global achievement gap: Why even our best schools don't teach the new survival skills our children need and what we can do about it*. New York: Basic Books.

Warlick, D. (2006, February). *Happy birthday jude*. 2¢Worth: Raleigh, NC.

Wiggins, G., & McTighe, J. (2005). *Understanding by design*. Alexandria, VA: ASCD

Wurman, R. S. (2002). *Information anxiety*. New York: Hayden.

Zittrain, J. (2008). *The future of the Internet—And how to stop it*. New York: Yale University Press.

Web Resources

The 21st-Century Fluency Project—*www.fluency21.com*

CourseSmart—*www.CourseSmart.com*

Electronista—*http://www.electronista.com/articles/10/03/08/verizon.says.lte.faster.than.rivals.in.practice/*

Internet World Statistics—*http://www.internetworldstats.com/stats.htm*

Wikipedia—*http://en.wikipedia.org/wiki/Crowdsourcing*

Wikipedia—*http://en.wikipedia.org/wiki/Marc_Andreessen*

Index

R

S

T

U

V

W

Y

21st Century Fluency Project

Also Available by the Authors

Understanding the Digital Generation:
Teaching and Learning in the New Digital Landscape

Today's world is different for our children. The technologies we take for granted or simply don't understand have become a part of our children's identities. This digital bombardment is shaping who they are and who they will become. We must realize they live in a different world, and speak a different language. Explore the characteristics of the new digital generation, and how education can be modified to enhance their learning experiences while supporting both traditional literacy and essential new 21st Century Fluencies.

www.understandingthedigitalgeneration.com

The Digital Diet:
Today's Digital Tools in Small Bytes

Andrew Churches, Lee Crockett, and Ian Jukes cook up a tasty treat for the digital newcomer in the entertaining and informative *The Digital Diet*. This book offers bite-sized, progressively challenging projects to introduce the reader to the digital landscape of today. This is the world of our children and students. *The Digital Diet* will help readers shed pounds of assumptions and boost their digital metabolism to help keep pace with these kids by learning to use some simple yet powerful digital tools. This is a must-read for your first dive into the world online!

www.thedigitaldiet.com

21st Century Fluency Project

Now Available on DVD

Living on the Future Edge
The Impact of Global Exponential Trends on Education in the 21st Century

Does it ever feel like our society is always in fast-forward? Are you frustrated by the experience of technologies becoming obsolete almost immediately after they're introduced? Do you struggle just to grasp how quickly and relentlessly things are changing? There's no doubt our world is on the move. The exponential changes and advances in electronics and online culture that we have witnessed in recent years have been staggering, to be sure. It's sometimes difficult to grasp the very nature of change, since it all seems to be happening so rapidly. More than ever it is a state of being that we struggle to keep up with as we live our everyday lives.

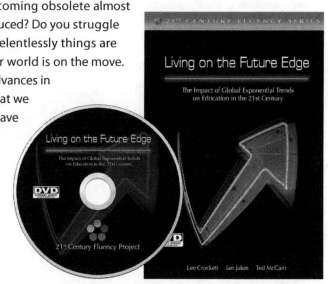

Living On The Future Edge provides a pragmatic look at the powerful and pervasive impact rapid digital evolution has on our way of life. This DVD presentation covers the exponential trends that are affecting our world and shaping our future, and clearing a path to tomorrow where the changes we are facing now can truly and benefit us all.

In *Living on the Future Edge* we see a fascinating time already in the making. It puts us directly into the expanse of an astonishing digital future that is coming at us at light speed.

To purchase this DVD visit:

www.livingonthefutureedge.com